MY LIFE SO FAR

MEMOIRS OF NICOLAS GAGE

Henry Nicolas Gage, 8th Viscount Gage

Dynasty Press Limited
36 Ravensdon Street
London SE11 4AR
www.dynastypress.co.uk

First published in this version by Dynasty Press Ltd.

ISBN: 978-1-9161317-3-6

Cover Design by Rupert Dixon

Typeset by Biddles Books Ltd., Castle House, East Winch Road, Blackborough End, King's Lynn, Norfolk PE32 1SF

Photography by ARW Photography and Dylan Thomas

Printed and bound in the United Kingdom

Contents

Foreword

In this book, Nicky Gage describes his father's memoirs as 'masterly but short'. The same could be said of his own. Both when being funny – which, again and again, he is – and when being serious, he has a gift for economy of style. Take this chapter opening:

'Sadly, the sexual revolution of the 1960s passed me by, as I was either sitting on my tractor looking after sheep or occasionally visiting my parents – whose butler disapproved of my agricultural attire.'

These words cram so much fact and feeling into a single sentence, and ensure, from the opening 'Sadly', that the reader will laugh.

Yet 'perhaps' the word 'masterly' is not the right one for Nicky. He is too modest for it. He is also too liberal, in the best sense, to want to master others. He is the exact opposite of a 'control freak'. He loves freedom of spirit and mind, and is happiest when he can help friends, family and neighbours exercise those liberties. It is hard to imagine him saying, 'Don't do that!' or 'You must do this!'

His stewardship of Firle, the place he loves most of all, shows this benign tolerance. Although he would never boast of it, this quality is very rare in the over-money-conscious, over-crowded and over-regulated Britain of the 21st century. Nicky's care for Firle – the place, its people and his family's 500-year role in it – is what unites this story and makes it moving.

Without being tediously confessional, Nicky is direct about his own failings. One of these, he thinks, is that he took much too long to grow up. Is that such a failing? No doubt it caused some difficulties along the way, but his childlike quality is central to the charm to which all his friends testify. It has allowed him to stay open to the world. He became a father in his seventies and continues to paint and hunt in his mid-eighties, an age when most men would long have put aside such things. He possesses an invincible innocence, which lights up his blue eyes, and makes this book a delight.

Innocence is not the same as foolishness. 'Human nature,' he writes in this book, 'possesses a sort of fragility that makes being the same person at all times rather complicated.' That is a wise thing to say. There is much wisdom in these pages.

Sir John Gage made the family fortune in the first half of the 16th century. Nicky, his descendant, writes admiringly of Sir John's good intentions towards Firle expressed in his will. We should all admire Nicky's fulfilment of those intentions in the 21st.

Charles Moore

This book is dedicated to my sons,
Ben, Henry and Valentine.

Acknowledgements

I AM INDEBTED to the following, who have helped me in various ways to compose this memoir:

Mrs Louise Flind, whose dogged enthusiasm has kept me up until the finish.

Mr Christopher and Mrs Primrose Arnander for their timely corrections.

Countess Caroline Cranbrooke for scholarly advice and for sending me a picture of Moel Brentoch.

Mr Christopher Whittick and Miss Deborah Gage for historical advice.

Mrs Helen Aitken, my old secretary, who corrected my grammar.

Baron Moore of Etchingham for his delightful introduction.

My wife Alexandra and my son Valentine for gallantly listening to my reading.

Introduction

I PLEAD NOT GUILTY of egocentricity in writing this short Memoir. True or not, the intended purpose is to wrack my depleted memory, and being egged on by my friends to bridge the gap of knowledge between the known past and the present future. Then the leadership of Firle will be taken over by my children.

Not so many of us remember the war years, fewer still the pre-war years: so snippets of information may be of value, as my late father's memoirs have been to me. Many years ago I had a dream that I was returning to Firle and being shown round as a past incumbent somewhat condescendingly. When I tried to pull rank I offered my bored guide a drink. I summoned my non-existent butler who had once occupied the back kitchen and noticed to my horror through a window the unmistakable appearance of a parking ticket machine - as the whole house had become offices and a wedding venue. Thank God this was just a nightmare. This contrasts with the precise instruction of our forebear Sir John Gage, who left Firle in his will to his eldest son and then to his second son in the hopes that whoever lived there would have the means to do so and love the house as much as he once had.

I hope Sir John's wishes will always be honoured, which is the purpose of this Memoir.

Nicolas Gage

Chapter 1
Early Times

I WAS BORN at Firle Place in 1934, in a house that would not have been much changed since the days of Queen Victoria and the early 20th Century, when it still had a considerable staff. An ancient member of that staff, Mr Hudson, who had helped my father conduct slightly dangerous chemical experiments and had engineering skills, was still working and making fireworks for the bonfire. A particular variety was called a Sussex rouser, which seemed to follow one about before exploding and would nowadays be considered to break every health and safety rule. Apparently, the midwife delivering me, mistaking a weekend guest for my father, congratulated Buns Cartwright, a quintessential bachelor and erstwhile famous England Cricketer, on having a healthy baby. Buns was considerably astonished.

My earliest recollections are of Firle, of a mouse running up the curtains in the Green Bedroom, and of riding a donkey in a sort of pannier with my brother Sammy on the other side. Though he was older than me he was lighter, and needed a pack to balance the pannier. I also remember cutting my finger on my mother's paper knife in her drawing room upstairs (now the Italian Room, and open to the public) when I was about three and a half. As a rule, we lived rather secluded lives upstairs in the nursery, and were only paraded downstairs to our parents from time to time. When my sister Camilla was born in 1937, my parents presented her to my brother Sammy, who was enchanted, but when my sister moved, he left the room yelling, 'It's alive!'

We had a remarkable, intelligent and totally selfless nanny, Nanny Rayward, who looked after Sammy, Camilla and me. She was the daughter

1

of a bookseller from Tunbridge Wells. All three of us owe a tremendous debt to this highly principled and redoubtable lady, who was such a constant figure for so many years. She remained a member of staff from 1932 to 1975, when very sadly she was placed in a nursing home, and I've always felt guilty that we let this happen. During the war she became a substitute mother. She dedicated her life to us, read T. S. Eliot, and was a central figure in our lives.

I vaguely remember hiding in an enormous oven used by Kingey our cook, in the old kitchen, now our tearoom. I remember walking down the street and meeting Mr Scovel in the Firle Stores, and with my Nanny buying sweets from a morose shopkeeper called Mr Matthews. He seemed to be permanently in a bad temper and had a bedraggled moustache. His shop is now the Estate Office.

When the Second World War came in 1939, we heard about it on an interminable train journey to Whiteslea Lodge, my Desborough maternal grandfather's bird sanctuary in Norfolk. I think I remember my nanny looking very serious on hearing the radio announcement by Neville Chamberlain, saying that we were at war.

I have very happy memories of Whiteslea Lodge and it deserves a mention, as it is a completely idyllic extended bungalow surrounded on three sides by the Norfolk Broads. Its particular location is in Hickling Broad. It was inherited by my uncle Ivo Grenfell (whom I never met) and transformed by my Desborough grandparents into a very comfortable villa, with walls decorated by dozens of original John Gould hand-painted lithographs of birds, pictures pillaged from one of the actual copies. The sitting room was ornamented by an oil-painted frieze depicting Hickling bird life – bitterns, hen harriers, bearded tits and varieties of duck – painted by the local artist Roland Green, who lived nearby.

To get anywhere we travelled by punt over long expanses of fresh water. Hickling Broad, interlinked with other broads or fresh water lakes, has a legendary beauty – vast areas of shallow waters divided by reeds in which novice punters can easily get lost. Enormous flocks of every aquatic bird assemble at different times, and the wild-fowling was conducted by a notable keeper, Jim Vincent, and his assistant Mr Piggin. I remember being shown a bearded tit's nest and excitedly listening to the boom of the bittern. I remember searching for plovers' eggs on muddy islands, and seeing my mother and a friend capsize in our sailing boat called *The Pochard*.

As we grew older, we became adept at punting and we visited Whiteslea regularly until the death of my grandmother in 1952. Eventually my mother sold it, as the upkeep of cutting back the reeds was considerable, but as always with my mother it had a happy ending as she sold it to the Cadbury family, who have been looking after it impeccably ever since, in association with the Norfolk Naturalists Trust.

During the first few months after the outbreak of war nothing much changed at Firle, apart from the arrival of Southover Manor School, evacuated from Lewes in case Lewes was bombed. My brother, Sammy and I attended Art lessons, and I remember a film in the Great Hall and making a rabbit carved from pumice stone.

My father had fought in the First World War and was wounded at Loos with a bullet near his heart. For some reason he was on active service at the outbreak of the Second. Both my parents seemed to rush about. My father apparently went over to France during the Dunkirk evacuation, when everyone else was coming back, but as small children we too seem to have been kept on the move. Finally, in 1940, when the fear of a German invasion was at its height, we were evacuated from Firle, spending some time with my parents' friends, the Hornbys, at their house in Pusey, near Oxford. My father took an executive decision against sending us to live with a distinguished American branch of the Gage family in Kansas, who had offered us accommodation. The head of the family there was John B. Gage, who was the clean-up mayor of Kansas City after the previous mayor Tom Pendergast had been arrested for dishonesty. The story of his corruption formed the basis of the novel *All the King's Men* by Robert

SOUTHOVER MANOR SCHOOL, LTD.,

LEWES, SUSSEX.

Firle Place,
Nr.Lewes.
November 30th, 1939.

Dear Lady Gage,

Thank you for your letter and cheque, for which
I enclose a receipt from the school.

I have had a talk with Miss Borland about the little
boys' piano. She is tentative, of course, of making
any very definite statement at this extremely early
stage, but she believes both boys are musical but that
Nicky has the greater aptitude and taste for it. It
is possible that he may have a more artistic make-up
than Sammy, as Miss Raikes said to me yesterday, " I
believe Nicky to be an infant genius!" when she was
talking of his drawing; but the trouble with these
things so often is that the turn or flair in a young
child becomes exploited and does not survive after the
child is 14 or 15. Miss Raikes is very anxious to
show some of their work to Mr.Henry Moore next term
when he comes down to examine and criticise the girls'
work, and I hope that you will allow her to do this.

About their piano lessons, Miss Borland says that
quite definitely the two little boys should not be
working together at the piano now, as Nicky is really too
young, but Sammy could attack his work at the instrument
rather more thoroughly, so you may agree to letting the
little boys have separate lessons next term.

About French, I am afraid I cannot help. I have
heard Mrs.Fuller well spoken of, and if she would come
out to you twice a week that might be a very good plan,
but I could not employ her in any way or put her up, as,
of course, we are very short of space. I am, however,
increasing my language staff next term, and although I
can not spare anyone to teach away from the school, I think
I can arrange two half-hours a week here, or possibly
a little more, and the little boys would have this quite
themselves with my teacher, as, of course, even the

Art Teacher's Letter

4

Penn Warren, which won the Pulitzer Prize in 1947. J. B. Gage visited Firle years afterwards with his charismatic wife Marjorie. He was an impressive American who was a personal friend of President Truman. Very many years later my sons Henry, Ben and I visited Marjorie in Kansas City, and she told me in an apologetic way that she had been the eighth best woman tennis player in the US in 1919.

My father decided instead to send us to an unknown but delightful Welsh couple, Mr and Mrs Dick Cadwallader (she was always called Caddie) in a remote village called Llanfair Caereinion, a little way from the market town of Welshpool in Central Wales. My father's options were evenly balanced – the danger of being torpedoed in a boat on the way to America or the possibility of England being overrun by the Nazis. His decision to send us to Wales proved ultimately correct, and Nanny Rayward was adamant that we should never leave England. As if this frail woman could singlehandedly withstand the Nazi invasion.

I have no idea what my parents did during the eighteen months we spent in Wales, as we never saw them. Our first cousins, Rosemary and Julian Salmond, had been evacuated to a house nearby, and a more distant family member by the name of Aylmer was around as well, as were some other cousins, the Meades, who lived down the valley from Llanfair. My brother, sister and I, and our nanny, had a delightful time with a governess called Truth. I played football with the local kids and climbed a small mountain called Moel Brentoch. We lived so far away from the outer world that the lookout post scanning the skies for enemy aircraft saw only one plane in the eighteen months, which turned out to be a friendly one. But for the Battle of Britain things would have been different.

Fourteen years later my climbing of a minute local mountain, which seemed very large as a five-year-old, stood me in good stead. When interviewed at the War Office Selection Board (WOSB) about my hobbies, I dangerously added mountaineering, only to discover that the officer was a serious climber and asked me what I'd climbed. I mentioned Moel Brentoch, which was too small for him to have heard of, but also a fact that he did not want to admit. "Good chap," he said, and I passed the interview.

In 1942 my father retired from the Army and became involved in the Special Operations Executive (SOE), where he worked in a secret organisation sending disinformation to Germany, including spying, sabotage and helping local resistance movements. It was known as Churchill's Secret Army or the Ministry of Ungentlemanly Warfare. Apart from working with highly intelligent people – Julian Amery, Dick Crossman, Fitzroy Maclean and Paddy Leigh Fermor were all members of the SOE – he never spoke of what he did, because of the Official Secrets Act. Nor did the others, who had pledged to the oath of secrecy and kept silent long after things were no longer secret.

Also in 1942, we left Wales and settled in St. Christopher's, an Eton housemaster's house in the High Street, and lived there for eighteen months. My brother and I attended St. George's Choir School in Windsor as non-singing day boys, and my father, who went every day to London from Windsor station, dropped us off on the way. This was a change from Wales – a more organised life, but pleasant all the same. My mother became a social success with the Eton masters and their wives, and occasionally entertained. She was befriended by Grizel Hartley, the legendary wife of the House Master of Baldwin's Bec, who herself was a scholar much loved by all who knew her and the heroine of a book by Rosamond Lehmann called *Dusty Answer*. She became a life-long friend.

I went on bicycle rides when not at school, developing a fascination with the local rubbish dump where a son of an Eton master called Mr Weatherall and I collected lead; but unlike in Wales we were more aware that a war was going on. I remember seeing pictures of the war in an exhibition in Windsor. Miraculously we escaped the bombing ourselves and I suppose the worst of that was over by 1942, but we had a siren just outside our house and a V2 did land in Grizel Hartley's garden, breaking all the windows but otherwise doing no harm. The arrival of Kingey, who cooked for us, with her daughter Deidre, who later became my sister-in-law, was a warm relief, since my mother could only cook rice puddings. Being rather idle she generally made ten rice puddings at a time, which we then had to eat for the next two weeks.

Travel was fairly restricted by petrol rationing, but we did make sporadic visits to my grandparents' house, Panshanger, near Hertford. This was an immense, rambling Victorian Gothic house with fake battlements, set in a magnificent park. Sadly, it no longer stands – like so many houses a victim of unnecessary pessimism in the 1950s. After the war some owners felt that their houses would be too expensive to restore, along with their way of life.

Panshanger looked like an enormous battleship, and contained a huge picture gallery. At one end, displayed on a red velvet background, was an enormous equestrian portrait by Rembrandt, and at the other an equally big Van Dyck. On the walls there were Van Goyens, Fra Bartolomeos, and at one time two Raphaels, the larger panel which my grandmother apparently sold to the famous art dealer Duveen, who sold it to Andrew Mellon, a very distinguished American art collector, and which now

Panshanger, circa 1850

hangs in the National Gallery in Washington. The smaller Cowper Madonna was bought by Joseph E. Widener, an industrialist and major figure in horse racing. There were a Pannini or two, one of which might have had fungus sprouting out of it. But this was the war, when it was seldom visited, so I as a child was the sole admirer. Panshanger housed one of the finest Old Master collections ever assembled, amassed by the 3rd Earl Cowper, who inherited his grandfather the 1st Earl of Grantham's collection of Dutch and Flemish paintings. Some of these were from the Dutch Royal Orange family, including the Rembrandt equestrian portrait and the Van Dyck. The 3rd Earl Cowper added Italian paintings, and his son the 5th Earl Cowper added Dutch and Flemish. The 7th Earl added more Italian and 19th Century pictures, such as G.F. Watts and Henry Fuselli, so the collection was an amalgam. Also, through marriage, came the Melbourne Collection, and the Van Dycks were moved from Wrest to Panshanger and hung in the dining room by the 7th Earl, and moved back to Wrest after his death.

Panshanger had a huge melancholic charm and overlooked a Repton Park. After my grandmother died in 1952 the collection was distributed between my aunt and my mother, the sole heirs. The Repton Park was pillaged by successive gravel companies, and the entire history of the Cowper family, my grandmother's forebears, sadly evaporated. Many of the paintings were sold by Christie's on 16th October 1953. The furniture was removed and, when no solution was found, the house was finally dismantled except for the orangery and the stables. A sad day. My grandfather's house Taplow Court still stands in Maidenhead, and the Desborough memory at least remains there, beloved by the Japanese Buddhists who now own it.

William Cowper, the 1st Earl, was the architect of the Act of Union of England and Scotland in 1707. The title survived for seven generations. The 3rd Earl lived mainly in Florence, and, with the help of his portraitist and friend Johan Zoffany, it was he who amassed one of the finest collections

Taplow Court

in England, including the two Raphaels. Some of the collection are now at Firle.

My grandfather Lord Desborough was a war correspondent and, in 1888, faced the enemy armed only with an umbrella. He was a famous athlete, and won an Olympic silver medal for fencing in 1906 when he was fifty. He was a brilliant organiser, and within eighteen months raised the money to finance the 1908 Olympic Games held in London and build the White City stadium. He became a Knight of the Garter for his services to sport. He swam under the Niagara Falls and, when someone disbelieved him, he did it again, surviving both times. He also excelled in many other activities, including boxing, running and rowing (he was a Double Blue and rowed with an Eight across the channel in four hours, twenty-two minutes), climbing the Matterhorn and three neighbouring mountains in eight days, and winning innumerable punting prizes (he latterly became known as Father of the Thames). He had married Ettie Fane, who later became a famous Edwardian socialite.

My grandparents suffered the appalling misfortune of losing two sons in the First World War, Billy and Julian Grenfell – a war poet best remembered for his poem "Into Battle" – and their third son, Ivo, to a car accident. They lived in frugal splendour in the enormous house. He lived downstairs, surrounded by his Ben Marshall and Zoffany, and his enormous collection of cups and medals, and a stuffed pike. He kept a loaded .303 rifle under his bed in case he ever saw a German.

When I knew my grandmother she was in her eighties, and was no longer the terrifying hostess of the interwar years. She read to us, played with us, and she and my grandfather were warm-hearted and kind. My grandfather died in 1945, my grandmother seven years later, bedridden but uncomplaining, surrounded by her loyal staff. She has had a book written about her called *The Intimate Life and Dauntless Spirit of Lady Desborough* by Richard Davenport, was visited by Winston Churchill during the war, and far from being a terrifying Edwardian hostess she didn't frighten us in the least, and we chose to spend our holidays with her. Her staff: Mr Barrett, Miss Lear, Emily and Yvonne and Miss Gaskell, were all devoted to her. We ate with them in the Servants' Hall, except for lunch, when we were trundled out to eat with our grandparents in the dining room, with their old Chow under the table.

Lunch was ritualistic, the food sparse because of rationing, and was cooked by the two former scullery maids Emily and Yvonne. My grandfather always mentioned that the cider came from the Zuiderzee, was somewhat monosyllabic and, though benign, for some reason often referred to bimetallism — of which we didn't understand a thing. Having been a great fisherman in his time, he was also given to casting with an imaginary fly.

I went to Highfield Prep School in 1943, by which time we had moved to Bushy Lodge (more of which later). In his autobiography, *On My Way to the Club*, Ludovic Kennedy has encapsulated the tense atmosphere at Highfield in one memorable chapter. In an awful way it was rather a good school. Canon Mills, the headmaster, was a charismatic but Victorian figure who beat most of us from time to time. He shamelessly helped himself to the boys' rations. Once, for snobbish reasons, he invited my parents to dinner and included me, and I then saw for myself the generous helpings of meat he ate when normally we would have been given a third as much. All were rather influenced by the dominant Canon Mills, who we nicknamed 'Bug'. There were at least two or three outstanding and charming masters, one a Mr Cavanagh and an enlightened French master, Mr Dixon. Amongst my school friends was John Leon, later to become a well-known actor with the stage name John Standing, Christopher Aberconway, and Garry, the present Lord Runciman. It so happens that the school bully lives locally and has since become a friend. His eccentricities remain and he's called Sir John Blaker.

My father apparently fared worse at his private school, St. Peter's in Seaford, where beatings were even more frequent. His fellow pupil Sir Sacheverell Sitwell said my Dad was picked on, but nobody knew why. I believe his nickname at St. Peter's was 'Grubby Gage', because he had an olive complexion. Eton afterwards was a wholesome relief.

In 1944 there was immense secrecy surrounding Firle Place, which was full of soldiers preparing for D-Day. The South Downs were used as a firing ground and the park was barred to visitors. On one occasion a bomb landed close to our house, but only a fox was killed. We were not allowed even to go into the park, let alone to Newhaven. Hence to this day, every time I go to Dieppe I think: How wonderful!

Mention should be made of the Home Guard, charged with saving Sussex from possible invasion. This comprised our rotund farm manager, whose girth was so considerable that when undertaking the army crawl there was little discrepancy in silhouette than if he was walking. Another unlikely member of the Home Guard was Duncan Grant, the famous artist who, on account of being a conscientious objector, had worked as a farm labourer during the 1914-18 war for the present John Hecks' grandfather. Duncan Grant had changed his mind sufficiently to join the Home Guard in the Second World War, but in his time with them carried a gun that was incapable, I believe, of using any known ammunition. The Hecks family are among the most revered members of our tenant farming community, each of whom is the life-blood of the Estate. The present John Hecks' grandfather died recently aged 99, a previous master of the fox hunt. Other members of the Home Guard were our Land Agent, Dennis Bush, and the present John Hecks's father, who told me that if any Germans came, the sight of them all might have caused the enemy to laugh too much to be capable of fighting.

Apart from the horse life, my father had a very extraordinary shoot which consisted of a rather surly game-keeper and a syndicate comprising my father, the Vicar, the Reverend Brown — who had been an erstwhile fast bowler for Sussex — the art critic Clive Bell, whose Labrador dog Smut was completely uncontrollable, and a very glamorous Scots Guards officer called Ian Henderson, who occasionally rode at Plumpton Races. He had been accused by the stewards at Ascot for winning a race at large odds, a win that could only have been achieved by pulling back the horse at previous races.

My mother, rather unusually for that period of history, was quite hands-on as a mother. She read to us, making us learn the Catechism for some reason although she herself was not religious, played with us, and taught us to ride. Exceptionally beautiful, she was the rather spoiled younger daughter of my grandmother Lady Ettie Desborough, who had had such a gilded life before her sons were killed in the First World War. She was funny, irreverent, prone to temper fits before 9.30am, capricious and far-sighted. Alas, she missed her mother Ettie, who had died in 1952, and was somewhat overwhelmed by my father's courageous decision to move back into Firle Place in 1948. It was requisitioned during the war and had been left in a mess by the army. Unlike Lady Desborough, my mother was no leading Edwardian hostess.

When I got to Eton as a pupil in 1947, I was reunited with my brother Sammy who had been at a different prep school. The war was over and life became much more enjoyable. Although intimidating at first, with the fagging and the duty to learn the names of the houses and house colours in the first fortnight, Eton had a sort of bonhomie that Highfield lacked and, though stressful, life was exciting. Having previously lived in Eton as a child, I had a slight advantage. My housemaster Nigel Wykes was enormously talented, both intellectually and athletically. He got a First at Oxford, and captained Essex at cricket. Behind a tense and unrelaxed manner, he was a very gifted botanist and lepidopterologist.

Eton was full of idiosyncrasies, so different from the Eton of today where there is no fagging, beating, boxing, early school, or the safety net of the stupid boy (students even less academic than oneself). These days everything is immensely well maintained, political correctness rules, and there are no eccentric masters like Herbert Hartley — who was so vague that he cycled over a courting couple on the footpath while coaching the Eight.

I was neither stupid nor clever, and I surmounted the Eton ladder fairly easily, ending up as House Captain and a member of the Eton Society known as Pop — an exclusive society to which most Etonians hoped to be admitted. This required a practice of ingratiating oneself to the Eton Society members (known as "Pop oiling") – sadly, a practice still needed today to get into selected London Clubs. I embarrassed myself so much by being obsequious to those in power that I decided I would never do it again. I think I have kept my promise.

In 1952 the Eton Chronicle had a competition and a small prize was given to anyone who wrote the best epitaph to the existing members of Pop. One such epitaph was of Henry Prior, a charming friend of mine who we had nicknamed Fud.

> *"Fud, nipped in the bud. Some worm will have a tussle*
> *to get through that great heap of muscle."*

Someone wrote a very rude one about me:

> *"In this pansy tomb Nicky Gage lies enshrined,*
> *a victory of charm over muscle and mind."*

Luckily my embarrassment was reprieved when my own epitaph won the competition, writing about my late friend Ben Whittaker:

"Here lies Whittaker.
Ineffectual, intellectual,
social cricketer."

It's not Eton's fault that a lot of Etonians never psychologically leave Eton. There is a very rare charm hidden in the historic architecture, now embellished by modern splendid buildings funded by the huge contributions of old Etonians. There is a feeling of expansion of horizons built by limitless self-confidence. My friend and contemporary Robert Loder was then precociously sophisticated and was a great influence on me and represented the above.

After an interval of sixty years, my wife Alex and I were shown round Eton in case Valentine, my youngest son, might go there. I hope something of this spirit still survives and has not been overtaken by earnest political rectitude. Nowadays the drawing schools, which used to be scruffy but creative, are magnificent but unnaturally neat new buildings (I believe the studios of great artists are notoriously untidy).

Many Etonians became friends for life, most of whom survive today, but sadly some of my greatest friends, George Christie and Robert Loder, have died. Thanks to George Christie, whose father John was my father's neighbour, I was invited to Glyndebourne while I was at Eton with George. I will never forget a production of Mozart's *Idomeneo* with, I think, the design by Oliver Messel, made remarkable by a monster which occasionally broke down.

The Christie family have historically been close friends of our family. John Christie taught my father at Eton before they both fought in the First World War. He was immensely kind to us children, and his wife Audrey encouraged us in the plays we put on at Firle. John, the founder of Glyndebourne, was himself extraordinarily eccentric, his eccentricity extending to driving us as children on the wrong side of the road from

Brighton to Lewes. Thankfully petrol rationing had eliminated most other cars.

Cosmo and Rosemary Crawley, who at that time lived at Ringmer Park, had become close friends of my parents, and their daughters Sarah, Camilla and Henrietta, were about our own age but seemed to be infinitely more sophisticated and glamorous than ourselves, and we were intimidated but bewitched by them. We grew up together and as children played almost every week. We learnt to dance with them, as their family always seemed to have the gramophone on, and they were part of our daily lives until National Service separated us. As adults we remain friends to the present day.

Seventy years later I have discovered a large cache of letters written by us as children to our parents, each painstakingly supervised by either our nanny or teacher. My brother Sammy's letters were beautifully hand-written and informative, and in reading them it is sad to observe that his earlier happier disposition became misplaced. He was undoubtedly affected by a car accident that he had when driving late to London, where he was studying film-making. The accident affected his vocal cords to the extent that he could no longer make himself heard in a crowded situation. Both my parents made valiant but unsuccessful efforts to understand Sammy, who retreated after National Service to become a world-rated eccentric. They adored my sister Camilla, who outshone us in every way, leading a self-disciplined life with a successful career as wife, mother, gallery owner, and confidante of the well-known and famous, but my brother had become a natural rebel. He eschewed social life and the 'upper classes', but retained an endearing charm. He once went to a local debutante dance and instead of thanking his host muttered audibly: 'pompous idiot'. When he joined the army, doing National Service, he was given the question: 'Why, Gage, do you want to be an officer?' at the crucial War Office Selection Board interview. Instead of the usual spiel of wanting to lead men, he merely said he didn't….. which surprised his interviewer.

Before I went to the army we were taken to Trouville by my parents and met the glamorous young McEwans and the very pretty Amabel Yorke on a motor launch organised by her father, Lord Hardwicke, who was the quintessence of an English peer. We had a very rough passage back in this converted motor torpedo boat where most of us were very sick, but during this time I developed an enduring attachment to Amabel, sadly interrupted by the brutal intervention of National Service. Around this time I often went to stay with the Barings at Field Place.

In 1952 I was called up to do National Service and earmarked to undergo training to become a Guards Officer. The Korean War was just ending. The initial square bashing at Caterham was like no other experience, a time when polishing boots became one's full-time occupation. We were so tired that when we were marched in to Padre's Hour, even before the Padre had spoken a word most of us were asleep, despite Sergeant Roley bellowing at us to 'get some f###ing religion into you'.

From Caterham I went on to the Officer Cadet Training School at Eaton Hall in Cheshire, which had to be tough as it was churning out young officers, some of whom were actually going to fight.

Eventually I became an officer, but not before I had endured a sentence of thirty-one days of Restriction, a punishment which consisted of compulsory parades day and night, on top of a very severe regime. There existed a parade drill order — which I think dated from the Napoleonic war — to slope arms and press the trigger five times. For some extraordinary reason I had managed to have a blank cartridge in the magazine, so on the fifth pull there was a deafening bang, and when my Commanding Officer yelled out: 'Who did that?' a trail of smoke issued from my barrel. I was made an example of, and I think my punishment of thirty-one days of Restriction existed as an all-time record at Eaton Hall.

After somehow surviving, I was commissioned as a Second Lieutenant in the Coldstream Guards and was posted to Krefeld in West Germany. We were fortunate that Colonel Arthur Fortescue ran an amazingly agreeable battalion and some fellow officers such as Mark Fitzalan-Howard who became friends for life. Another National Service Officer was the now notorious Lord Lucan, in whose innocence I still, rightly or wrongly, believe.

West Germany in those days was divided into four Allied Occupation Zones administered by the British, French, Americans and Russians. We made efforts to meet the local populace, and against the trend I had taken a few German lessons. On one occasion I had to welcome some local Krefeld worthies in my inadequate German. The all-night manoeuvres extended our stamina, but for an eighteen-year-old this was an exciting and maturing process. I remember going with a group to Wuppertal Air Base and being made thoroughly sick and frightened when we volunteered to be flown in jet trainers and the pilots showed off their skills, much to our discomfort.

In fact, National Service subalterns were not taken very seriously by the army, and quite rightly so, as I remember leading a convoy down a one-way street ending in a cul-de-sac.

From Germany I went straight to Oxford in 1954 and read History at Christ Church, a famous Oxford College where I shared beautiful rooms with my cousin Robin Gage in Peckwater Quad. Compared with the army, Oxford seemed less adult. Christ Church remains one of the most nostalgic places on earth, but without the fixed military regime it was an easy place to lose one's bearings and to daydream, aided by the wonderful array of architectural gems, and 'dreaming spires'. Prelims was a tough exam which I thought I had definitely failed but actually passed.

My memories of Oxford are vivid: being taught by Hugh Trevor-Roper; much average port being drunk; the discipline of producing essays on time; once representing Oxford in a boxing match (my uncles Julian, Billy and Ivo Grenfell were Blues – I not); and attending *débutante* dances in London and driving down well over the limit and breaking into Christ Church in the early hours. They remain poignantly strong, as do many other memories of misbehaviour, such as painting zebra stripes on the road outside Christ Church. However, I spent some time at the equally beautiful Cambridge where I visited Robert Loder, and in particular Caroline Jarvis, both of whom became friends for life.

As mentioned, one of my tutors was the eminent historian Hugh Trevor-Roper. In his memoirs, *Letters from Oxford*, he writes to Bernard Berenson about me. He says, 'Do you know some people called Corsini? I have a pupil called Nicolas Gage who is going to Florence in July to learn Italian and stay with them. He is intelligent and engagingly dotty – a dottiness which comes (I think) from his mother, *née* Imogen Grenfell, daughter of Lord Desborough.' Berenson replies that 'the Corsini are the most respectable family of Florence.' I also remember one time seeing a bulging file in Trevor-Roper's rooms which he had labelled 'Death to Tawney' – who was a much-respected rival historian.

Among the dons I was entertained particularly warmly by Lord David Cecil and Rachel his wife, and was once driven home very erratically by him having dined at New College. Through him I met a fascinating array of academics, including Sir Isaiah Berlin, Maurice Bowra, Dame Iris Murdoch and Dame Enid Starkey, who became a great friend of mine as we both enjoyed drinking together. The difficulty of talking to Isaiah was to furnish him with enough subjects on which he could expound, which he did so quickly that one ran out of subject matter. Maurice Bowra was a very genial host.

Oxford was an exciting place that on paper offered the enjoyment of absolute freedom — in practice it was quite a steep, testing experience as one is given enough rope to hang oneself. I enjoyed the spectacular beauty of Christ Church, and the cattiness of the dons making incredibly clever digs at each other. Speaking of a famous literary critic one don said: 'I regard him as a sensuous piece of blotting paper.' Another, speaking of a fellow don, said, 'That man's mind is that of an intelligent scholar's waste paper basket.' Evelyn Waugh's image of Oxford had a persuasive influence, where undergraduates sometimes acted out the parts which had never existed in the first place.

There was one enormously funny occasion when my future brother-in-law, Edward Cazalet, convened a hunting debate at Christ Church which was attended by well-lubricated undergraduates who boisterously 'crossed the room', alternately siding with a 'yay' or a 'nay' whenever a debating point was made, and especially after the very eloquent speech of the late David Wynne, who made twenty-five points for and twenty-five points against the motion. The chief speaker was Major Gerard, master of the Beaufort Hunt, who appeared to be somewhat ill at ease in an urban situation, and a fiery Greek, Constantine Mano; and against the motion was an anaemic vegetarian director of the RSPCA and an eloquent gay undergraduate, Hans Calmann.

I once hunted with the Heythrop, organised by Ed Cazalet — a fearless and very accomplished rider — where my horse Augustus unexpectedly gave a senior member of the hunt, Richard Fleming, a lead over a wide stream. On one evening I was simultaneously invited to box for Oxford, to dine with the eminent historians Hugh Trevor-Roper and A. J. P. Taylor, and to go to a deb dance. I should have tried to do all three, but predictably the deb dance invitation won the day.

I took advantage of my first summer holiday by going to Canada, where I had an exciting time with two other Oxford undergraduates, Peter Barnard and Ben Hanbury, and was entertained in Vancouver by a family friend. I worked as a deck hand on a tug boat going to Alaska. I stayed with the Governor General, Mr Vincent Massey, in Government House, and I was also furnished with a letter from the Governor General arranging for me to visit the studio of Lawren Harris. He was a member of the Group of Seven, a renowned group of 20th Century Canadian painters. This was indeed a unique privilege, but sadly I think I was too exhausted to have taken in this honour, having spent the day being an electrician's mate in a Vancouver dockyard in order to finance my holiday.

Back in Oxford, being a friend of a fellow undergraduate Fionn O'Neill had the benefit of being partially taken up by her charismatic socialite mother Ann Fleming, who seemed to know all the dons and at whose soirées the guests included politicians like Hugh Gaitskell, artists like Lucien Freud and Francis Bacon, and lawyers such as Arnold Goodman.

I think Oxford coincided with the sad episode of the Suez debacle, when a fellow undergraduate Angus MacIntyre was called up for some months for the possible invasion of the canal. The result was the procrastination and aborted invasion, and the loss of any chance of his claiming a first class degree. He incidentally was ordered to send out to Suez a midnight blue cummerbund which was the prerequisite of any officer taking part in armed combat.

I turned down the invitation to join the Bullingdon Club, which seems now, accidentally, to have been the right move. However, I still remember the ordeal of being the junior member of the Loder's Club, and having the dubious privilege of obeying the custom for junior members of having to finish off the Loving Cup — which normally contained, among other things, a bottle and a half of port. Next day I received a call from Lord David Cecil, who courteously asked me how I fared at the final exam. Unfortunately my state of health, as a result of the previous night, prevented me from remembering that I'd even taken it. This considerably puzzled him.

I suppose I had many opportunities and that it was a high privilege to have been at Oxford, but nothing there prepared me for a career decision. I was awarded a third class degree, and received a consoling letter from Hugh Trevor-Roper while in Istanbul during a trip to Persia with Terence Bendixon.

The Oxford degree system, where there is only one exam at the end of the third year, is a tough one. I would never have got a First, but might have got a reasonable Second if I hadn't lost my temper in the middle of School by misreading a question on Palmerston — described as the last of the Canningites — so much that in the later general paper I agreed with Henry Ford that 'history is bunk'. Looking back fifty years later I wrote the following, which was printed in the Christ Church magazine:

"On being told by a friend last year that we are all yesterday's men I replied that I have never been today's man so it doesn't matter."

Firle Place and Lord Gage

Simon Offen *(1986)*

The Right Hon. the Viscount Nicholas Gage came up to Christ Church to read Modern History in 1954. He inherited his titles and the magnificent family home, Firle Place, on the death of his brother in 1993, their father having died in 1982.

Lord Gage kindly invited the Christ Church Association to visit Firle this summer, and forty of us enjoyed the most idyllic of English summer days, with a splendid lunch in the local pub, The Ram Inn, a guided tour of the House, a walk in the beautiful gardens, and a champagne tea on the terrace. Nestled in the South Downs near Lewes, Firle must be one of the most beautiful estates in the country.

In discussion Lord Gage described himself "as a backwoods squire with a passion for the preservation of the countryside and an interest in being an amateur painter." His ambition is "to preserve as far as possible and within the bounds of benignity the status quo in East Sussex, where our family has resided for 500 years." Remarried a few years back, Nicholas and his second wife, Alexandra, have a son, his third, and judging by the

energy he displayed when showing us around I would not bet against the family being at Firle for another 500 years.

On painting, Lord Gage describes it as "an abiding passion, whether or not I would have been brave enough to have devoted my life to it, debarred by other responsibilities, is an open question." He continued: "Being neither very good nor very bad at anything has been advantageous, as it means that at the age of nearly 80 one can go on doing things, such as various aspects of sport, which a more perfectionist athlete would have given up long ago on the grounds that it would damage their reputation."

Of his time in Oxford he believes "there is no more nostalgic place on earth than Christ Church, and the danger of being beguiled is ever present. I remember being both utterly elated and also on occasions despondent as there seemed so little in the way of a safety net, but despite this I look on it with enormous affection, possibly more from the safety of old age."

And what of the pressures of being responsible for an historic House? Firle has just been entirely reroofed at huge expense. "Keeping an Estate and listed house has had the same sort of problems, on a smaller scale, than those that best the administrators of a mighty Oxford college! It requires steely determination, the ability to innovate, the tact of an experienced ambassador, and a degree of hard headed realism and chutzpah. Would the Dean and Governing Body of Christ Church agree?"

Champagne tea on the terrace at Firle

The Long Gallery

A portrait of Lord Gage

Lord and Lady Gage with their son John

Chapter 2

Growing Up

IN WRITING MEMOIRS, it is difficult to know how much to put in or leave out. My father's memoirs on his early life, including the 1914-18 War, are masterly but short. They conjure up the full horrors of the war in a brilliant, evocative but impressionistic way. He did not wish for them to be published in the family edition, but three instances I feel I should repeat here, hopefully with his blessing.

Once he saw a German, unaware that my father had his gun pointed at him. He was saved by my father's inhibition, not from any form of cowardice or compunction, but it had been drummed into him that he must never shoot a sitting rabbit. My father shot above him, and the German escaped unhurt.

In the final stages of the First World War, my father was severely wounded and heard his runner say, 'Right through his bleeding heart, he's a gonner.' My father was then carried on a stretcher by two captured German Prisoners of War, and it says much for his presence of mind that while being severely wounded he noticed that the Germans were taking him in the wrong direction, back to the front. He not only noticed this, but remembered enough schoolboy German to say '*Zurück*', which the Germans obeyed, carrying him to the safety of the field hospital.

My father was a modest but rather formidable man with a high intellect but an essentially feudalistic view of life. He was rather controlled by his eldest sister, Aunt Rene, who gave him consistently bad advice. He appointed an estate agent, Dennis Bush, of whose dominance my father appeared seemingly unaware. Nevertheless, he managed to accomplish a great deal. He championed local drainage as the creator of Seaford Defences. He was Chairman of the County Council, President of the National Housing Federation, chairing three hundred and fifty delegates from the 1950s to the 60s, and, because of his age was senior 'Father of the House of Lords'.

According to the late Dougie Bunn, the creator of Hickstead show jumping, my father, when chairman of the County Council Planning Committee, helped him by telling the Committee: 'Let the young man have a chance.' He remained witty, famously telling the Lords, when challenged by a Labour Peer in the Lady Chatterley case with: "Would you show this book to your wife?" that he would show it to his wife, but not his gamekeeper.

During training for the First World War it was usual to salute any superior officer. Allegedly, when challenged at Aldershot by a Major in the Sussex Regiment as to why my father, a Lieutenant in the Coldstream Guards, had not saluted him, my father replied: 'I'm a Colonel in your regiment.' Indeed, he was an Honorary Colonel in the Sussex Guards.

Perhaps my father's most lasting achievement was the preservation of the South Downs. Between 1933 and 1937 the planning was under the exclusive right of Eastbourne and Brighton and Hove district councils, in which the East Sussex County Council had representation but no vote. There was a dispute about the use of a motor racing track at Portslade, which later was passed to the House of Lords. In 1937 my father was chairman of the Town Planning Committee, and he used his influence to draw attention to the landlords, which included the municipalities, to prevent unrestricted building on the South Downs by raising general awareness of the problem. This was a lasting and immensely beneficial contribution to the preservation of the South Downs, now in the hands of the National Park.

Throughout my life Firle has had a central role. My parents were old-fashioned and shocked by staff costing 100% more than before the war, yet they hadn't made the modern adjustment of living in the kitchen, so the statutory four meals a day were brought on silver trays to the dining room. But at the same time economies were made in the quality of the food and wine, which were well below average. I think they were dominated by their staff, and fearful in case they left. My father gave everyone a particularly poisonous white wine, so that no one ever asked for a second glass.

This did not stop my parents entertaining on a fairly generous scale, and the great and the good did come from time to time, especially for my father's shooting weekends. It was customary for the house guests to be woken with cups of tea in the morning. Our then butler, Mr Frost, had a particularly neurotic wife who knocked on the door of my parent's guest Nancy Lancaster (who had famously entertained in her various houses, Ditchley being one of them). Mrs Frost asked whether she could do anything for her. Nancy Lancaster replied that she was doing her teeth, to which Mrs Frost responded by asking if she could do them for her. Nancy Lancaster, recounting the story to my mother, said: 'That's service for you!'

Another of my father's butlers, Mr Powell, once approached Caroline Jarvis when she was staying at Firle and told her that the house was thronged with ghosts, and that they made such a racket at night going up and down the main staircase that they kept my mother awake, to the extent that she had changed her bedroom. He then went on to say that if Caroline met him at midnight under the stairs, she too would see the ghosts – an invitation she did not accept.

We owe a debt of gratitude to all staff over the last forty years, which include Penny and Peter Woolgar (whom I mention later), and Sue and Cheri Rolfe, who fed us and kept the house for us for so many years, looking after my parents, my brother and latterly myself. Penny is still cooking for Alex and Valentine and I.

My brother, who had been to the agricultural college at Cirencester, started an eccentric dairy farm close to Charleston, home of the Bloomsbury group, where he addressed his farm manager as Mr Cater — and the farm manager addressed my brother as Sammy. When he wasn't night clubbing in London, Sammy had a puritanical streak and used to milk about fifteen Jersey cows at 5am. Later on in the morning he would invariably have coffee with the artist Duncan Grant, who lived at said nearby Charleston. He once brought back an entire band from the Stork Room, a London night club in Swallow Street, to help him with the morning shift. When Duncan Grant lent Sammy a picture he had painted for the Cunard Line, it was too big to get in through the door of 'Peaklets', the cottage where my brother lived next door to Charleston, and Duncan allowed the picture to be sawn in two to enable it to be displayed there.

My sister Camilla, who for some unknown reason didn't go to university, where she would have flourished, went to America to work for the Financial Times in New York and became the 'Belle of the City'. Camilla has been and continues to be a great support in my life.

My parents lived rather separate lives, my mother getting up late, drinking a bit, and then riding in the dangerous local drag hunts. My father pursued his corporate duties in the County Council, National Housing Federation and the House of Lords, but his patrician, measured life style was a contrast to my mother's wild and slightly unfulfilled nature. She was a keen competitor in the local horse shows, riding side saddle and being coached by the renowned horse showing expert Sam Marsh.

Having left Oxford, I was encouraged by my aunt's husband, Ernest Tennant, to enter the City. It was with a feeling of considerable apprehension that I went into an apprenticeship with the established trading company known as C. Tennant Sons and Co of 4 Copthall Avenue, a rather dapper building in EC2 which housed a hundred or so staff.

C. Tennant had been a go-ahead business in the 1920s. The original Charles Tennant had sired two daughters in the 19th Century at the age of eighty-one and eighty-two, and had been the inventor of bleach, a patent sold to ICI. When I joined, I believe that the Chairman, Lord Glenconnor, and I were both economical with the truth. I told him it was a job I'd always wanted, when in fact I wanted to leave as soon as possible; and he told me that I would have security for life. Its days were indeed numbered when I joined. Despite boasting the prettiest secretaries in London, in the '50s the firm was in decline, and the mercurial Lord Glenconnor's brilliant but maverick son Colin sold it to Consolidated Goldfields. With hindsight I should have gone to Flemings, where the managing director was a brother of my famous trustee and godfather, Peter Fleming the travel writer. But I was too wet to go against my father's wishes as his sister was married to Ernest Tennant, who was the elderly co-chairman of the company.

At that time a girl I was rather fond of suggested I should farm, and sadly when I did so I isolated myself from London, resulting in not being able to pursue our relationship. I am however grateful for her advice. The day I left the City, and the reason why I did so, was probably the most important and life-changing decision in my life. As mentioned, my anxiety to carry out the wishes of my father and his sister Rene, in a pathetic desire to please, explain why I got into Tennants. My departure, when I was somehow made to feel ignominiously as if I was letting down Queen and Country from a job I should never have accepted in the first place, was another story. My decision was not exactly cowardly, but nevertheless panic and claustrophobia drove me to hand in my notice. I packed my bags and moved down to Fawsley in Northamptonshire.

The Fawsley Estate was left to my father in 1934, as my father's grandmother was Sophia Selina Knightley and the future Knightleys were childless. The Knightleys had lived there since the 16th century and although it was one of the grandest estates in Northamptonshire my father never much cared for it. I think he had bad experiences of it when sent up there as a child, as he had to stay in the big house under Louisa Knightley

— who he liked — and also in Little Fawsley, which was inhabited by Lady Juliet Knightley, wife of Sir Henry Knightley, who he detested.

As a second son I inherited the Estate, which was passed on to me in stages and was heavily Trusteed. I went against the Trustees and my mother, who wanted me to choose an independent estate agent, which I eventually did years later. Instead I retained the existing estate agent, Dennis Bush, and as a result spent ten years of farming drudgery, as pedestrian as it was worthy.

Fawsley Hall was architecturally impaired by an addition of two Victorian wings by Sir Rainald, who became Lord Knightley in 1892 and who wished to impress Queen Victoria, which he did at the expense of selling a large acreage of his enormous estate. He was so conceited that contemporaries changed the hymn words of Joseph Addison's Evening Hymn from:

> *Soon as the evening shades prevail,*
> *The Moon takes up the wondrous tale;*
> *And nightly to the listening Earth*
> *Repeats the story of her birth:*

to:

> *And Knightley to the listening Earth*
> *Repeats the story of his birth:*

During the two world wars the house was occupied by the army, and was further damaged by the agent Dennis Bush letting it to the Over Timber Company, which resulted in piles of sawdust piling up in the Great Hall and, worst of all, one of the finest timber roofs in the county being removed and replaced by a modern structure.

Before the war my father had sold the unique stained glass in the Oriel Window to the Burrell collection in Glasgow. It is said that Sir William Burrell called this acquisition the best piece of business he had ever done.

I nearly bought the house in 1960, but good sense possibly intervened. The fact that it has now become a thriving hotel can be ascribed to the entrepreneurial talent of Ted Saunders, who bought it and lovingly repaired it, and my own interventions. I admired Ted, but successfully prevented him from changing Fawsley into flats. In my capacity of Chairman of the Fawsley Meeting I had previously prevented Turriffs from building executive houses in the grounds, and so the final result was the creation of the 5-star Fawsley Hotel. This is the best solution for stately homes whose owners find them too expensive to live in, a far, infinitely better result than the fate that befell my grandmother's house in Panshanger which is, as reported, sadly demolished.

I initially lived in Little Fawsley with the agent's son Paul, but although Dennis Bush had put his son into a farming tenancy — strictly speaking a conflict of interest — I struck up an unlikely friendship with Paul Bush, who years later was awarded an OBE for his services to the disabled. I also gained farming experience under his foreman, a splendid Sergeant Major type figure called John Trotman.

Fawsley Hall (now a hotel)

I lived a solitary bachelor life, went to Moulton Farm Institute, drank a lot, worked moderately hard, rode with the Pytchley and Grafton Hunts, and was occasionally entertained by the hunting fraternity. For some reason I felt compelled to lead a lonely and isolated life, which was occasionally relieved and enlivened by weekends with my father and mother, the odd London dance, and the generous hospitality of the Birkenhead family. It was a self-made purgatory as a result of my damaging City experience, from which I very slowly returned to normal. On reflection there were amusing moments — once I persuaded a sophisticated lady to go out with me in my beaten-up Renault 4 car, and she suddenly emitted a scream, as she thought she'd seen a mouse. After the evening had ended I put a mouse trap in the car just in case, and found that it did in fact catch two mice.

In leaving Tennants, where I naively believed one of the Director's predictions that I would never live this down, I developed an inferiority complex. As a result I attended Northampton Technical College in the hopeful attempt of achieving two A-levels in chemistry and botany in six months - a feat that would have tested Einstein - in order to get a place at Reading College, which I was convinced was the best place to go. Instead I went to Moulton College, which had no such requirements and was a most peculiar and healthy experience, and more down to earth than can be imagined. Moulton was a result of meeting the head lecturer in the Dun Cow pub in Daventry, where Paul Bush and I were having a drink.

Looking back fifty-five years later I'm struck by the extraordinary timidity I seem to have been afflicted with. When all my other friends were getting engaged, married, having children and climbing their respective ladders, I was fumbling with chickens and pigs. This period of my life was a reassessment of previously held values and a sort of second childhood. There was also the camaraderie of the fiercely competitive Pytchley and Grafton Hunts, as they both hunted over the estate and had been warring over this shared domain for more than a hundred years. I managed to solve a particularly vicious argument between the two hunts by remarking that I had not been consulted as a landowner. Immediate peace broke out, but heaven only knows what I would have said had I indeed voiced an opinion.

The respective masters Peter Borwick, and Colonel Lowther and Colonel Foster, set standards of which all of us were much in awe. I met countless hunting friends, including the McGowans and the Cazenoves and many others, and dined regularly with Mrs Whetstone — who lived in a completely Jane Austen setting — and Lord Wimborne and the rest of the hunting fraternity. I learnt a lot about the different respective social patterns of Northamptonshire and Sussex. Northampton was essentially more self-contained and county based, and Sussex much more international and London orientated. I think the combination of being educated first at Eton and Oxford, and later by Moulton Farm Institute, were salutary — the dreaming spires replaced by total earthiness.

Moulton consisted of very basic but useful instruction. Its pupils came mainly from the farming community, intermixed by a few 'gents' who wanted to do a crash course in farming. It was a humbling but beneficial experience, as all sense of social superiority vanished when demonstrating prize bulls in front of the local farmers, some of whom hunted with Pytchley. It had some notable past pupils, including Lady Mary Dunn, Frankie Donaldson who was the wife of a socialist peer, the late Lord Salisbury, and Connie Jarvis, mother of my friend Caroline Jarvis. I was also astonished to find that another pupil was George Hartigan, who had previously been a Cambridge scholar. As an experience it was infinitely worthwhile for a year.

The late F. E. Birkenhead, reputedly the cleverest man in England and who became Lord Chancellor, had adored my mother, and my father had been his private political secretary. His son Freddie Birkenhead and his wife Sheila, both authors, held court in Charlton Manor, and I spent many evenings there thanks to my friendship with his son Robin and his daughter Juliet. Robin would hold court like an enigmatic King Arthur in Camelot with his many friends, who included Susie Aird, Roddy

Bloomfield, Annette Bradshaw, Jacob Rothschild and Stuart Wheeler, all of whom were heartbroken when he died in his forties. A masterly account of the life of Winston Churchill between the years of 1924 and 1940 by Robin Birkenhead was privately published posthumously.

I had weekly forays into the hunting field on a horse that I looked after myself. It was a curiously cathartic period of my life, starting a new career. At the same time, I lived an extremely simple and impoverished lifestyle. As children we were brought up naively to believe that money was scarce, and this opinion was readily endorsed by the solicitors and estate agents who were probably lining their own pockets. Street wisdom was completely lacking in my father's otherwise formidable intellectual armoury. It took an embarrassingly long period for us to realise that one cannot be broke with a large amount of land; and for various girlfriends to understand that it wasn't parsimony but financial ignorance that my brother and I couldn't afford to entertain them in the standards they expected. It has to be said that my father was unusually careful about giving away or spending money.

Chapter 3

Middle Age

SADLY, THE SEXUAL revolution of the 1960s passed me by, as I was either sitting on my tractor looking after sheep or occasionally visiting my parents — whose butler disapproved of my agricultural attire.

After attending Moulton, my life at Fawsley from 1960 to 1965 was spent in the incredibly boring occupation of fulfilling the 5-year programme of the long since abolished 'Small Farmers Scheme'. On my small holding of thirty acres at Fawsley I laboriously underwent the steady programme of fulfilling so many 'man hours' on farming associated stock. I've forgotten the exact calculation, but each cow, each pig, each sheep, and each chicken required so many 'man hours' to shepherd and look after. A tiny grant was awarded on a yearly basis, after an inspection by the authority. It was a means whereby an apprentice farmer could achieve competence in a 5-year period. It was an immensely dull way of gaining farming experience, based on a book called *The Farming Ladder* by George Henderson.

Weekly forays with the Pytchley hunt on my horse Augustus broke up the monotony. On one occasion before hunting I remember feeding Augustus with pig nuts — having run short of oats — when the Master Peter Borwick was out; and that day Augustus jumped out of his skin. Many years later the local horse-mad farming family the Tarrys looked after my horse. They were and are an immensely shrewd, unsophisticated family and their son Jimmy was unconventional to say the least when winning two hundred or so races in point-to-points and over the sticks. Father Tarry (Bunny) is still an amazing character aged ninety, and I have spent many hours hunting with him and exercising his terrifying horses.

Edward and Camilla Cazalet, Mr Bonar and myself riding 'Augustus' prior to Grafton Cross circa 1970

My parents were aghast at my solitary behaviour, but put a brave face on it. Thanks to my brother-in-law Ed Cazalet, on one weekend I took part in an old-fashioned point-to-point race where one was supposed to take one's own line over natural fences — as an equivalent of the old-fashioned races where there were no organised jumps as there are in the modern point-to-point race course. It was started by the legendary Colonel Foster, who I always thought looked like Captain Ahab, and who put down his flag shouting: 'God be with you'. We all finished, but apparently my brother-in-law, who would normally win such a race, on this occasion did not because he gallantly reined in his thoroughbred when his wife-to-be crossed the path in front of him.

The hunting fraternity were very kind to me, and I had numerous dinners with Sandy Chain, Liz Ward and many others. By and by, after attending various painting night classes and a City and Guilds farm accountancy course, I graduated to a bigger farm on the estate, and slowly built up the momentum to take charge of running the whole Fawsley Estate. I think the process of wresting control of the Fawsley Estate stood me in good stead when, many years later, after my father and brother had died, I eventually became the incumbent of Firle; and finally dismissed the agent who had been running the estate for fifty years and began to organise financial matters so that the habit of selling cottages at every opportunity in order to balance the books was discontinued.

My mother died in 1969, and I still feel her loss. She had such an amazing childhood, and had been so much adored by so many famous suitors, but she was rather unfulfilled. We should have supported her more. She could easily have afforded a London house in the 1960s and 70s, but she lacked the confidence to do this, and was also discouraged in this extravagance by my father. Although she had many friends, some much younger than herself, and she rode fearlessly with the formidable drag hounds, she lacked the steely willpower and social ambition of her famous mother Lady Ettie Desborough. She might have been happier in the less formal surroundings of Bushy Lodge. As previously described, the Grenfell family, of whom my mother was the youngest, were victims of the hideous 1914-18 war.

When my mother died my father was lionised by his partnerless contemporaries until he finally surrendered and married Diana Cavendish, a very different character from my mother but whom my mother had liked. After the initial culture shock of only coming to Firle on my stepmother's invitation, I grew to like her immensely and she genuinely loved my father. They endearingly had their photographs taken by the society photographers Lenaire. Then it was Diana's turn to entertain her grand friends, who included her sister, the formidable Betty Salisbury, and the late Mary Roxburghe, along with Diana Cooper, who was a much more interesting and famous friend and had been a leading 20th century beauty. She was very fond of my esteemed war poet uncle Julian Grenfell, who was killed in 1916, and his brother Billy. She later married Duff Cooper, the diplomat, politician and author, who was a critic of appeasement and the 1938 Munich Agreement before the Second World War. I believe she was mentioned in a F. Scott Fitzgerald novel, and she personally told me: 'I am a living legend and I'm not up to it.' Actually she was well up to it, and never without a male companion.

I simultaneously moved from the flats to the cottage at Charwelton and had acquired a flat in Dolphin Square in London to enable me to attend the Byam Shaw School of Art. The changes of life at Firle occurred concurrently with a huge alteration in my own life when I married an attractive wild-child: Lady Diana Beatty, eighteen years my junior. Diana's grandmother was the daughter of Marshall Field, whose wealth was so colossal that when her husband — the future Admiral Beatty of Jutland fame — once inadvertently rammed his destroyer on a rock she reputedly told the Admiralty that she would replace it at her own expense. I met her with Sir Sacheverell Sitwell and his wife Georgia, who, I believe, were targeting me towards Diana's widowed stepmother.

I was brought up in a drinking culture, as was my new wife. When I married I was almost a virginal bachelor, whose agricultural pre-occupation was at odds with a fun-loving 60's child whose parents had been divorced and re-married many times. I was too slow to adapt, my wife too impatient, and after our two wonderful children Henry and

Ben were born, despite mutual affection we found ourselves living very separate lives. Our relationship was further endangered by the potential poison of lawyers. I was financially naive, Diana would say parsimonious; while she was fun-loving and hedonistic.

*Lady Diana Beatty
and Henry*

She did introduce a regime change at Firle, creating a modern kitchen, much to the dismay of Peter and Penny, as it had been their stronghold. Peter and Penny had exercised a profound but beneficial influence on the upbringing of my older sons, Henry and Ben. Despite Peter's somewhat autocratic disposition they have been a source of security for my children for which I am very grateful.

For the next twenty years we lived in and out of a form of marriage with our poor sons, whom luckily we loved and looked after, tagging along behind us and putting up with our successive dalliances. Both of us were to blame when Diana finally divorced me, after which I felt a sense of vacuum until, to Diana's horror, I met my present wife Alexandra thirty years later. Whereupon my mental dexterity improved due to the curtailment of half my previous intake of alcohol.

At that time I had the responsibility of looking after Diana's mother, Adelle Dillingham. She was a very glamorous, thrice married, ageing American beauty, whose personal charisma was matched by her extraordinary naivety over anything financial. She had recently lost a fortune by buying African tribal art to be shipped over to America, where it sold at a huge loss. In New York she took a lease on Nijinsky's studio apartment in the Hotel des Artistes on the West Side, which was very atmospheric. Once I drove her past Harry's Bar while she was explaining world poverty to me, and when I remarked that dining at Mark Birley's establishment cost at least in excess of £200 a head, she replied that she thought this was extremely reasonable. She may not have been very practical, but she was indeed good fun. She stayed for some time in my London flat in Dolphin Square.

According to some historians Sir Thomas More was a man for all seasons. I suppose that is a quality that we all ascribed to, to be equally at home with a beggar or a duchess. However, human nature possesses a sort of fragility that makes being the same person at all times rather complicated. A few incidents in my own life show how impossible it is to maintain the quiet English sangfroid. One when I was asked to play football by the Byam Shaw school of art team and had to cross White's Club in football clothes, dreading being seen by my conventionally attired fellow members. More recently, as a church warden I was instructed by the local school mistress, who was herself a church warden, to march in a procession round the church, carrying a lighted candle to mark the Feast of Epiphany. Her excitement was such that she decided to continue the procession outside to the graveyard, and this unfortunately coincided with a meet of the drag hunt, who looked extraordinarily nonplussed to see a figure cowering behind the gravestones holding a lighted candle and praying to the Almighty that none of the drag hunt members would recognise him.

Another incident happened in the House of Lords when I walked across the front bench to greet a friend, which later required a lot of grovelling to the Minister. Even more embarrassing still was my speech at the house of Mrs Slocombe, the doyenne of Newport Massachusetts, at a dance given to celebrate the marriage of her grand-daughter. The story goes as follows: An American ex-girlfriend's son was marrying into the Slocombe family. I had spent a night at Boston airport owing to bad weather, and I arrived jet-lagged the next day. After the wedding party, where everybody was wearing dinner jackets, I was suddenly asked to say a few words. Amongst the audience were members of the Kennedy family and John Carter Brown, the famous director of the National Gallery of Art in Washington. The result was a predictable disaster, so embarrassing that I'll never again be able to return to the glamour of Newport. Hell hath no fury like a woman scorned.

Chapter 4
Old Age

My father died in 1982, aged eighty-six. Thereafter, there was a family discussion as to who would live at Firle Place, which was complicated by the fact that my poor brother Sammy at that time expressed no desire to live in the house as he was frightened of the ghosts. I volunteered to do so, and for a year my stepmother, whose relationship with my brother was at zero degrees, consented to stay on temporarily.

Diana and I hovered around Firle while my stepmother hung on, jealously overlooked by my brother who was living and farming nearby. Eventually my brother's animosity won, and my stepmother moved back to Cumbria where she already rented an attractive little house from her nephew, Hugh Cavendish, who nicknamed it 'The Auntery', with her aristocratic widowed sister Mary Crawford living nearby.

Disaster overtook my marriage when during a holiday my wife began an affair with an erstwhile friend of mine with whom, to everyone's horror, she more or less eloped. She sold her smart London mews house, partially owned by me, and set up with her new boyfriend for ten years in a house she bought in Clapham. I then proceeded to live partly in Northants, partly in London in Dolphin Square, and most weekends at Firle, managing the 2,000 acre farm.

When my stepmother left, my brother, accompanied by his future wife Deirdre Kingsbury, moved slowly back into the house. A flat with independent access was carved out of the house for me and my children, and my brother and I then shared Firle, occasionally acrimoniously, for ten years until his death in 1993 — when his secret marriage to Deirdre was announced at his funeral.

In 1971 Sammy had indeed married. He had been living totally happily with a pretty but retiring girlfriend Anne Dutch when my father, and possibly my sister, thought that the affairs of the heir to Firle should be regulated, and persuaded him to get married to Anne. It was vital that I should attend this ceremony, even though I'd endured the misfortune of having recently interfered in a dog fight, with the net result of having lost a bit of my index finger. The service was a peculiar affair. At the point when my brother said to his wife, "With all my worldly goods I thee endow," my father whispered audibly under his breath, "If the trustees agree." Subsequently the union was bent on disaster, and sadly the couple's marriage was dissolved in 1975 on the basis of non-consummation. Poor Anne Dutch who came from a respectable middle-class family was pensioned off in a very economical fashion, which later made my brother very proud. Having attended this peculiar ceremony I returned to Northants, and next day was confined to hospital for fourteen days as a result of the poison to my finger occasioned by the dog bite.

Much later my brother and Deirdre, the daughter of Kingey, had become close. We had all been thrown together during the war when she became a family friend. She had become a qualified piano teacher and worked for the United Nations, and she looked after my brother devotedly. Later she secretly married him. After my brother's death in 1993, she very generously passed over much of her inheritance to the Gage Estate for the benefit of future generations.

My dear brother Sammy and I had a genuine love-hate relationship. He really loved the village and he rebelled against what he considered the pretentiousness of the upper classes, dressing in impoverished clothing and helping to wash up in the restaurant. He loved telling the trustees how poor he was at the meetings, to which they all, possibly for financial reasons of their own, readily agreed. He regarded me with fondness, mixed with a partially justified contempt for my financial profligacy, but as he spent no money of his own he saw things from a biased point of view. When he died, he put in his will that I should in no way benefit financially.

But he had a good side. He loved dressing up as Father Christmas and entertaining the Firle schoolchildren. He enjoyed lighting the Firle bonfire on the 5th November, judging the ankle competition and occasionally shocking the establishment by keeping the house in complete darkness while drinking bottles of wine. One of the reasons he disapproved of me was that he thought that I hadn't helped him sufficiently to sack the common enemy, the estate agent. That I failed to do this was by incompetence rather than non-cooperation.

I had become a trustee of The Henry Smith Charity, which is a worthy organisation that has distributed money for centuries. During my trusteeship I was seconded to the Housing Associations' Charitable Trust which occupied a fair bit of my time. When the Trust's other sources of income were failing, I like to think that my contribution via Smith's charities helped to ensure its survival to the present day, especially as its creation was partly due to the efforts of my late father. Its founder Henry Smith had bequeathed his farmland at Chelsea in the 16th century for the benefit of his kindred and the victims of Barbary pirates. By miraculous coincidence the trustees had benefited from the expansion of Chelsea, so that four hundred years later the charity distributed millions of pounds to a diverse number of beneficiaries. When I joined I particularly liked one of the directors who managed the farmland, but I disliked the directors managing the urban estates, and, being vague, I was unaware that the two branches of the firm had indeed separated some hundred years before. It was through ignorance rather than ill-intent that I let my brother down by not recommending who would have been an ideal agent for him, and thus deserved his displeasure, which merited his instructions to the executors.

I remember arriving at Firle one evening, as usual in complete darkness, when a curtain opened in the brushing room window, disclosing the butler Peter Woolgar squinting out at me. When I opened the kitchen door I was startled to see my brother also sitting in complete darkness, and, noticing my surprise, telling me that they always sat in the dark owing to the expense of electricity.

Occasionally, against all odds, I did give weekend parties, telling my guests that they must avoid my brother who was a recluse. All went well till one of my guests, having retired to bed, pressed what he thought was a light switch. In reality it was a bell to the old scullery which had not been operative for years, and my guest was surprised when the terrifying figure of my brother emerged in his dressing gown, furiously asking him if he required a gin and tonic.

I remember the upside-down sequences of this ten-year period, which included my entertaining the American ambassador, Henry Catto from Texas, who brought his American mother. The reason he wanted to visit Firle was because she was an American Gage. I was fearful of his meeting my brother, who might well have asked him why he was there. The ambiguity of my living in a small portion of the house and my fear of upsetting my brother — as there were stern notices to delineate my occupancy in the house — made my position untenable, and I was indeed about to leave Firle when he finally died in 1993. The night before he died, he instructed me to take antibiotics as I had a bad throat. He himself was suffering from appalling pneumonia.

In light of my brother's death, I no longer pursued my plans for relocation to a different house. Amazingly at about this time my wife, although we were divorced nisi, came back, and for the next five years we lived together, or at least shared the same house. In 1995 we gave a celebrated twenty-first birthday party for my eldest son Henry, coinciding with the five hundredth anniversary of Gages living at Firle. Limitless champagne and the Kanga Bonga band led to innocent but tipsy behaviour. When I went to bed I found three guests sleeping peacefully in it. They politely left, and the next day were found sleeping on various settees while the tent was being demolished.

This mirrored the enormously successful party that my parents gave in the Long Gallery for my sister Camilla's 'coming out' party in 1956, when there was dancing in the Long Gallery to Ambrose & His Orchestra, who had been very successful in the 1930s. It also mirrored my own eightieth birthday party in the riding school, which was followed by my wife's fiftieth birthday party, as successful and splendid as any previous party. And when my second son Ben was recently married to Natasha Llewellyn at Firle by the Firle vicar, the Rev. Peter Owen Jones, it was followed by a large luncheon party in the Great Hall which everybody enjoyed immensely — overcoming the potential danger of having three Lady Gages, none of whom were on speaking terms with each other, in the same space.

My brother never took up his seat in the House of Lords, but I did so in 1995. Diana helped me write a maiden speech, a testing experience. Although believing in the continuation of the hereditary principle, in a regrettably increasingly politically correct atmosphere I was never really enamoured of political life. I attended nearly once a week, made two or three speeches and asked two or three questions, but though stimulated by the completely unexpected entrée into main stream politics I wasn't fully committed to it.

Political divisions in The House of Lords are much more muted than they are in the House of Commons. My father recounted me a story of a Labour Peer getting up and cheerfully saying: "When your Lordships were huntin' and shootin' I was shuntin' and tootin'."

I had met Lord Callaghan at a ploughing match dinner at Lewes Town Hall, therefore I was rather shocked that when I went up to shake his hand it was withdrawn with icy disdain. The next peer I happened to meet was the late Dennis Healey, who I accordingly passed off without recognition, wrongly thinking that habits at the House of Lords were similar to that of the Commons. I was told afterwards that he was rather hurt. Later we became very good friends. He and his wife cooked us lunch at his house in Alfriston.

I never dared to take part in a big boy debate, when some of the best brains in England are engaged, although I regret not taking part in an asylum debate of which I knew a little owing to being a trustee of the Housing Association Charitable Trust. Asking questions at 2pm when all the old ennobled Prime Ministers attend is a truly terrifying experience. On one occasion when I spoke, had I not met my highly articulate friend Caroline Cranbrook (formerly Jarvis), who coached me for five minutes on my question just before I was due to speak, I honestly think I would have spluttered to a standstill. Afterwards Hansard made my contribution quite impressive in their account of the day's business.

Once I sat on a particularly inviting and empty bench when a friendly peer whispered that I was on the Bishops' Bench and if one appeared I should give way. I spent the rest of the afternoon perching on the very end of it.

I like to feel that I made two contributions which have had a beneficial effect. One was the requirement for animal feed compounders to declare precisely from where their products originated. I remembered that in my farming days mad cow disease was thought to have come from infected bone matter put into the feed by the manufacturers. As a result of my question in the House of Lords the *Farmer's Weekly* praised me after one of the compounders, Dalgety, agreed to do so. Secondly, I hope my contribution pointing out that church repairs necessitated a VAT charge, which I outlined in my maiden speech, helped to gain the rebate that is now available to churches throughout the land.

In the 1999 reforms I put my name forward to say that I would be happy to spend two days a week in the newly constructed House of Lords if elected. Those elected were expected to attend every day, and only ninety-three hereditary Lords were allowed to remain. I submitted my desire to continue, but was duly excluded along with the majority of hereditaries. It had been a wonderful experience, but time consuming, and my rejection allowed me to concentrate on the Firle Estate and my desire to be an amateur painter.

Regarding my subsequent permanent marriage break-up, blame was again equally divided. I felt outmanoeuvred by Diana's strong advocacy to sell a family chattel, a Fra Bartolomeo, to the Getty Museum in California in order to provide an endowment for Firle. My heart disagreed but my head said yes, and a valuable and beautiful family heirloom was sold for £14 million (after tax £7 million). Although the wisdom of it was subsequently proved to be justified, I had meantime made life difficult for Diana, who bolted after we took a successful holiday together in Colombia. We had walked to the Lost City from Santa Marta, and it took two days of torment from mosquitoes for us to be amply rewarded by visiting one of the most beautiful parts of the world. But I was again left alone. Oscar Wilde's view that youth is a priceless gift far too valuable to be squandered on the young particularly applied to myself and my then wife Diana. In our case the joint growing up process of both of us somehow got delayed to late middle age. However, now is the time to look forward and not back, but, before I do so, I need to describe my relationship with Firle and the responsibilities that its ownership brings.

Sir John Gage, General Gage, and possibly my late father, were ambitious enough to gain national recognition. Unlike them and my friend and neighbour George Christie, who rebuilt Glyndebourne Opera House and has based his memoirs upon it, I am more representative of all the other Firle incumbents who have been content with being good landlords, the preservation of the countryside and the continuation of the five hundred years of Gage history. Firle has been a full-time career for me, as it has been for most of my predecessors: many other incumbents simply busied themselves in the preservation of the estate and welfare of the village.

Some of the Firle village was rebuilt to give employment in the slumps of the early 19th century. However, the fourth Viscount was so reactionary that he was opposing the Reform Bill long after the Duke of Wellington had accepted it. Firle village, with its pub, school, vicarage and shop, creates a lively community and a refreshing benchmark against the terrifying conformity, rules and regulations, and absence of privacy that are the hallmark of the 21ˢᵗ century.

In France the Code Napoleon is completely contrary to the English custom of primogeniture. Whatever the ethics of this custom, it has kept landed estates intact with many beneficial results. The collections, or works of arts, can be displayed for the benefit, not only of the family but also for the many thousands of visitors that share in the beauty of these objects and of the house and countryside when they come to visit Firle. It has also benefited the villagers, some of whose families date back to the time, or even before, of the arrival of the Gages in the 15ᵗʰ century. However Firle, no longer challenged by the invasion of Hitler or Napoleon, faces new threats from political rectitude. Sussex uniquely honours the bonfire tradition.

In the year 2000, my cousin Debo Gage and I attended a re-enactment of the American War of Independence at Concord. The Battles of Lexington and Concord were the first military engagements of the American Revolutionary War. We got up early, arriving at Lexington Common at 6am where the first shots of the revolution were fired on April 19ᵗʰ 1775. I had the duty of inspecting a thousand Americans dressed as English soldiers, which I did to the best of my ability as I hadn't inspected any troops since my National Service forty years beforehand. We were rewarded the next day by meeting the modern day descendants of the main American participants of the war, which included the posterity of Samuel Adams, Thomas Paine and Paul Revere – who was a lawyer from Marblehead. I made a mental note that if I ever needed a lawyer in America I would appoint Paul Revere to act for me.

Also in the year 2000 my farm was invaded by travellers when the Firle Bonfire society, of which I am president, had the bright idea of igniting a caravan full of the images of travellers with the number plate P I K E Y. When a politically correct villager reported this to the Commission for Racial Equality all hell broke loose. A day later the whole village became filled with police. I was personally interrogated while walking up the drive, and fifteen villagers were arrested on the suspicion of being criminally racist. On the night in question I happened to be three hundred miles away, but nevertheless it was reported erroneously that Lord Gage was seen dancing and yelling: 'Burn them! Burn them!'

The following article was printed in the *Sunday Telegraph* in a successful gambit to bring the incident to an end:

Lay off revellers who blew up gipsy caravan on my land, says viscount

BY RAJEEV SYAL

VISCOUNT GAGE, whose land was invaded by travellers and then used by a local bonfire society to burn a model of a gipsy caravan, has called on the authorities to deal leniently with locals arrested for inciting racial hatred.

Police arrested 12 members of the Firle Bonfire Society in East Sussex last week after they burnt the wooden travellers' caravan complete with models of a gipsy family inside – which had been inscribed with a number plate that read PI KEY, "pikey" being a derogatory expression for a gipsy. A group of travellers had recently spent three weeks on nearby fields owned by the Gage family.

The arrests have caused uproar in the village of Firle – population 200 – and has upset Lord Gage, too.

The Commission for Racial Equality has also become involved, and has called for the police to take the matter seriously.

In his first interview since the row began last week, Lord Gage, 69, said that the incident had "gone too far" and called on the

The caravan, containing models of a gipsy family, is blown up at Firle

police and others to show common sense. "I hope the powers, having the whole event has gone off into made their point and distracted us the realms of fantasy," he said. with the matter. It was just a bit of over-exuberance. The village, which is absolutely charming, has got into the headlines and that is just what Firle has avoided for 500 years," he said.

"There wasn't any real or con-

trived malice in the bonfire. I think the whole event has gone off into the realms of fantasy," he said.

The travellers that prompted the row arrived on the Firle Estate in August – the first time that it has been invaded in the 500 years it has been under the Gage family's ownership.

The travellers upset the locals so much, Lord Gage said, that he

decided to go and see them. "They were just taking the mick-ey, having a lovely time on other people's land, making a mess.

"They don't respect the land, they don't bring portable toilets or anything like that and make a hell of a mess, especially this lot," he said.

He said that he was surprised to find that they drove a number of plush vehicles including a Porsche. "I saw 14 caravans, a Porsche car, a pile of rubbish, a bit of human unmentionables [excrement] and a lot of scrap metal."

"A very smart woman came out of a caravan. I didn't talk to her because I was told that if you do, then they say that you have given them permission to be there," he said.

Three weeks later, after paying £2,000 to get a writ forcing the travellers to leave his land, he served it upon them. They dis-played a chirpy and engaging style, he said. "A charming Irishman came out of a caravan and said to me: 'Of course, we are going tomorrow. By the way, do you know anywhere else we

can go to?' Very cheeky, I thought," said Lord Gage, the eighth viscount.

The Firle Bonfire Society, which dates back to 1875, held its annual celebration on Octo-ber 25. Members had painted images of a gipsy family peering out of a window on the side of the caravan, which was wheeled through the streets before being set ablaze. The police became involved after a local television news broadcast reported the incident.

Next year, Lord Gage will be ploughing more fields on his estate in a ploy to keep travellers off his land. "Travellers do not like ploughed land because they find it difficult to drive on to Next year, I will plough a few more fields," he said.

He will also take the precau-tion of finding out exactly what depict in its annual bonfire.

"I don't think the bonfire will be controversial in future. T the whole there is a very go atmosphere at the bonfire. Th year's event lacked finess that's all."

I have always painted part-time though, never daring to become a professional. Who can guarantee an income from it if Van Gogh couldn't? I remain a keen amateur painter, encouraged by Duncan Grant and the Bloomsbury connections of Charleston, created almost accidentally by my late father whose tolerant and intellectual attitude encouraged the arts. Duncan Grant, such a central figure in the Bloomsbury Group, settled in Charleston Farmhouse between the wars. He was a generous enthusiast to all aspiring painters and was never known to say anything rude about anyone's paintings.

I was occasionally allowed to paint in his studio at Charleston with my great friend Lindy Dufferin, who, as well as being a celebrated hostess, is a good painter — she paints as Lindy Guinness — and who was also a good friend to Duncan in his old age. We had enormous fun in his company and he kept us on our toes. I have painted regularly and spasmodically for at least seventy years, culminating in a successful one man show in London in 2018, and have been much encouraged by my wife Alexandra. The sensitivity required to be a painter is a limiting factor in the judgement required to be a success in other areas such as business or politics, but nevertheless, rightly or wrongly, it has remained part of my persona. It has also opened up other areas of aesthetic awareness. In fact, there is nothing in my life that I find more baffling and ultimately humbling than the act of painting, and this I did more intensely after my retirement from the House of Lords. With the help of a mysterious teacher called Adrian Baumgartner, who was introduced to me by my friend the cartoonist Nicky Bass, I embarked on an ambitious programme of self-motivating painting exercises. Adrian, whose talent I consider rather wasted in his pre-occupation with arduous self-discovery paintings, would have been happy in the Renaissance. He gave me the confidence to undertake large paintings – a process somewhat similar to making a jigsaw, as you cannot see the end of the picture for many days and weeks. Sometimes painters, and possibly writers, cannot see the wood from the trees, and need a truly talented tutor gently to point out a problem, encouraging perception and enabling one to carry on.

Due to the efforts of my cousin Debo Gage, Charleston Farmhouse has now become a much visited house museum. It has been immaculately restored, which would have amazed the socially retiring but very creative previous occupants. Famously the home of the Bloomsburys was often visited by the economist Maynard Keynes, who became a tenant at Tilton. It once became my lot to be guest speaker after an annual general meeting of the Preservation Society of Charleston. This seemed an innocent request, but having agreed to do so I was alarmed to discover the fame of the previous speaker, Lord Annan, renowned for his scholarship and eloquence. Luckily I was furnished with unique information and, thanks to the unstinting help of my articulate friend Primrose Arnander, I believe I managed to accomplish this task with credit.

The communication revolution over the last ten years has eclipsed the technical revolution that occurred in my father's day before and after the Second World War. The challenge of the preservation of the countryside and (forgive the cliché) the 'built heritage' is huge, together with the threat to Sir John Gage's mid-16th century perception of benign landownership. To my mind political correctness is a dangerous misconception, and would certainly clash with Sir John's enlightened and affectionately responsible care of the land.

Firle has always been a social centre, and needs to remain one. My grandparents on both sides of the family were enormously social. Instead of the coterie of statesmen such as Balfour, intellectuals such as Oscar Wilde and H. G. Wells, and The Souls, the group of aristocratic intellectuals, politicians and beautiful women who adorned the famous country house salons of Ettie Desborough, my Gage grandmother entertained minor German royalty at Firle. The stuffiness of the conversation and the repeated changing of clothes throughout the day and evening must have taxed the listener as well as the lady's maids. A close friend of my grandmother, Alice Salisbury, said that she told so many white lies that she could ice a wedding cake.

People and parties make Firle come alive, as the three large parties given by my mother, my first wife, and more recently my second wife have shown. My parents had many of their own society friends and relations to stay, though entertainment was limited for several years after the war by food and petrol rationing and my parents' terror of servants leaving. My mother had a slight inferiority complex for not being equal to her famous socialite mother, but still maintained a high standard. She was very good with the young, and we had endless children's parties with the Crawley daughters, who appeared very precocious in comparison to our naivety. We had great fun with George and Mary Christie who lived at Glyndebourne. My stepmother, Diana, came into her own and put in bathrooms and entertained intellectuals, bridge-playing companions and her aristocratic sister, Betty Salisbury, very frequently. She was amazingly competitive, and when I came to her for sympathy during my divorce she proceeded to demolish me at chess, bridge, backgammon and billiards in lieu of sympathy. I came to admire her for her uncompromising upper-class steeliness.

As a bachelor I entertained modestly, even though during this period Firle was enhanced by the visits of the Duke of Edinburgh and his entourage, who for several years used Firle as a launch pad for taking place in the carriage driving championship competition at Stanmer Park near Brighton. Micky Nevill helped me with entertaining him. During one of his visits my son Ben came into the downstairs drawing room and greeted a gentleman with the words: 'Hi man, I hear the Duke of Edinburgh's coming,' only to discover he was talking to the Duke himself. He retrieved the situation by saying that the Duke looked so young that he didn't recognise him.

As a result of entertaining HRH Prince Philip, I was on three occasions invited to stay at Windsor Castle. This was a particularly intimidating experience. In the late evening the numerous staff disappear, and on one occasion I had completely forgotten where my bedroom suite was. Had there not been a solicitous Lady-in-Waiting present I could have easily stumbled into rooms occupied by a dowager Duchess or a member of Prince Philip's royal relations. Thereafter I always marked my bedroom by locating its position in relation to one of the many masterpieces in the Queen's unique collection.

For some years I did have my own house parties and, on one famous occasion, encouraged by plentiful Château Léoville Barton, one of my houseguests disappeared after dinner to reappear having squeezed into the armour last used in 1839 by the son of the 4th Viscount at the Eglinton Tournament (a re-enactment of a medieval joust). Johnny Gathorne-Hardy

Event in Riding School circa 1890

*Picture of my late mother
Imogen Moggs circa 1930*

Camilla, my sister

Me and Camilla as children

*Lord and Lady
Desborough with my
brother circa 1934*

Nanny Rayward circa 1938 with myself (right) and brother Sammy

*My stepmother
Diana Cavendish*

Me, Henry and Ben

Lady Diana Beatty with Lord Beatty and Jack Fransis

*Aunt Rene (left) and
Aunt Vera (Right)*

*Moira Kennedy (nee Shearer)
and my father circa 1960*

Henry with Jeremy Quinn at his 21ˢᵗ Revolution Birthday Party

Rev. Goddard with H.M. The Queen Mother and my brother George John St Clere Gage (Sammy) at my sister's marriage to Edward Cazalet at St. Peter's Church, Firle

Adelle Dillingham

Me Eventing circa 1988

Mount Ararat which Alex & I climbed in 2009, with a little artistic license.

Still life at the Cottage, Northants

Alexandra Gage

Alex & Jupiter, Firle Place

Whiteslea Lodge

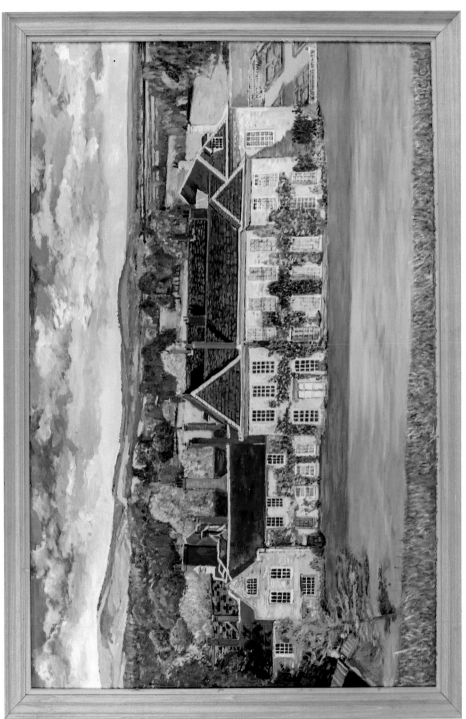

Firle Place

My mother from a Country Life photo 1936

Third Earl Cooper, famous 18th Century collector who lived mainly in Florence

Sir John Gage

The Hon Henry Gage
with kind permission of Dylan Thomas

Valentine, Alex and myself
with kind permission of Dylan Thomas

Lockdown 2020

Lockdown 2020

South Downs

cut himself severely when he shut the visor, and the armour had to be repaired at vast expense.

Firle holds a fascination to outsiders, but it isn't a particularly easy house to live in. It's very beautiful — John Julius Norwich in his 1985 book 'The Architecture of Southern England' described it as the most beautiful 'small' house that he knew — is slightly haunted, and, despite some large sales, is still a treasure house. The danger and the challenges for future generations are that it will become a museum and lose all its purpose of being a family home. This would be contrary to the wishes of Sir John Gage when he wrote in his will that he hoped that the future Gage incumbent would love the house as much as he had himself. He might well have added that the incumbent and his wife will require nerve, taste, business IQ — and generosity.

Firle demands feminine energy. I imitated my late father by marrying for a second time and this has proved a wise decision. Firle simply requires too much energy for one person, and a bachelor could be subsumed by the house, which is like a beautiful woman and requires constant attention. It has a curious effect of changing its inhabitants, which includes the family, the internal staff, butlers etc. and the guides, all of whom are subject to flights of fancy and the danger of being self-important. It's essential for the boss to exert authority (as opposed to pomposity) and keep everybody down to earth, remembering it's a space for living, rather than a museum.

Having never expected to receive the title or incumbency, I have always regarded myself as a curator, facilitating events in the house to provide income for its upkeep and repair. The financial commitments are enormous. For instance, the cost of keeping the roof in good order was £1.5 million just for part of it in 2009. This means that income from events is an essential pre-requisite, and the nature of the house will be forever changing. Firle hosts films, television programmes, dinners, visits from high court judges in a wing of the house, and weddings in the riding school.

The governance of Firle has changed in my lifetime. My late father was the last incumbent to have enjoyed absolute power. Nowadays the incumbent is first amongst equals, and decisions are made in committee. Thanks to excellent trustees this compromise has worked rather well, and because of their unstinting and largely unpaid work the estate continues to thrive. Much gratitude is also due to my cousin Debo Gage, whose equally unrewarded financial enthusiasm and love for Firle has kept the collection well looked after and appreciated by distinguished authorities worldwide. Thanks to all of the above and many others, the show goes on.

Further mention should be made of Fawsley, Firle's sister estate in Northants, which came through my father's grandmother, Sophia Selina Knightley. The life of the original Sir Richard Knightley mirrors that of Sir John Gage, who lie respectively in St. Peter's Church, Firle and St. Mary's Church, Fawsley. Curiously both Sir John Gage and Sir Richard Knightley were obliged to witness the execution of two royal ladies, Sir John that of Lady Jane Grey, and thirty years later, Sir Richard that of Mary, Queen of Scots. I spent twenty years of my life at Fawsley, and am delighted that my second son, Ben, is making its preservation his life work. Its Capability Brown park is immensely beautiful, though the house, now thankfully a hotel, is less beautiful, as it was compromised by the addition of a Victorian Wing due to a visit from Queen Victoria. The estate is indeed a poor relation but also a very beautiful one, and it boasts a remarkable ruined 16th century Dower House in Fawsley Park.

I asked my good friend Nicholas Baring to become a trustee of Firle, little knowing that I'd engineered the appointment of the most thoughtful, formidable and upright trustee, one who's proved to be a benign but steely disciplinarian. I'm glad to say we are still friends. Although my ego was dented, the combination of our different interests regarding the house has resulted in outright benefit to Firle Place. For instance, his thoroughness in insisting on a detailed survey of the house resulted in the discovery of a dangerous chimneystack, which might have collapsed at any time, just above the Van Dyck in the Great Hall. Thoroughness is a virtue, the absence of which I am occasionally guilty and which has resulted in errors of judgement for which I'm still doing penance till this day.

At the age of eighty-five I think one's allowed to moralise. One is also obliged to think of mortality, and I'm hopeful that life will be not dissimilar in the next world; that there will not be the torture so believed in by Dante and Hieronymus Bosch, but if one does not fulfil one's obligations in this world one will go into the next with the absence of brownie points. Throughout life I have been a churchwarden, for fifteen years in two churches. I do believe there will be an after-life and exactly the same problems will be there. The late Lord Donaldson, who had been a Labour Minister, was staying at Firle and insisted on going to Holy Communion. Despite being a double-first intellectual he confessed he didn't know what he believed in but Christianity was the best option. I share his view.

I have had lucky escapes: driving the wrong way up the M1 for thirty miles; falling into the Thames after slipping on the gang plank to my boat in Chelsea Harbour, only to be fished out barely conscious in the middle of winter; being barged off the A27 and forced through a hedge by a motorist driving without lights; being run away with on the Downs escarpment after the drag hunt had finished; and suffering a heart attack in Rishikesh in the Himalayan Foothills, where I spent two days in a local hospital, the Jolly Grant Hospital. No one there spoke English and I think I was the first European ever to have visited. The nurses were very sweet, and occasionally still send me cards. Women were not allowed to sit, and when my wife Alex kindly came to visit — her journey having been complicated by wild elephants — she arrived only to find that she couldn't sit. I was miraculously saved from an operation there by the luck of a connection with Virat Bhatia, the regional president of AT&T, whose intervention facilitated the organisation of a military jet to take me to a sophisticated hospital in Delhi where the surgeon was a close friend of Barack Obama.

The late Alan Moorehead, author of his book *Gallipoli* and whom I met on a Hellenic cruise with my family, suffered a horrendous stroke in later life. As a result he could only say four words 'bloody awful' and 'bloody marvellous'. This seems to be an accurate account of life, but so far my life has been more of the latter.

As everything has been said either by Shakespeare or Dickens, it is trite to give any word of advice to my successor, other than to say that honesty is a sort of insurance policy.

Chapter 5
Dotage

AN AMUSING BACKDROP to life at Firle is recorded in the memoirs of the part-time land agent, family friend and general assistant, Walter Ingram, who moved into Firle about the time that the 5th Viscount inherited it in 1877. My grandfather was twenty-one and Walter Ingram was twenty-six years old, well connected and married to a Sclater, the family who owned neighbouring Newick Park at that time. He lived in the downstairs apartment at Firle, alongside his employer, the 5th Viscount and his wife (who for some reason he called Mrs Gage), and other Gage relations who included Georgina and her sister Constance. He succeeded a dour agent called Mr Griffiths who had been apparently given notice and as a result refused to help.

Walter Ingram moved into the Black House in Firle where my father's agent Dennis Bush lived some fifty to eighty years later. He gives an account of the Firle staff, the gardeners, cooks and other staff, and seems to have controlled the Gages' spending, as Leila (Lady Gage) accused him of being a very hard man. History repeats itself, as his successor Dennis Bush strictly controlled my parents' purse strings sixty years later. In his diary Ingram allowed the cook half a pound of meat a day as a regular allowance, including the bone, and added that there were always rabbits and game in season, poultry and eggs, as well as the half pound of meat. My grandparents apparently lived some of the week in their London house, 41 Whitehall Place, which was occupied by a caretaker, and they took one or two of their servants with them when they went there. Walter Ingram tried also to control this house but seems to have failed in this respect. This didn't stop Ingram going to many dinner parties at Firle where he sat on the right hand of Mrs (Lady) Gage, who was prone to go to sleep. It was his duty to wake her up whenever there was a good dish on the table.

House parties, which Ingram seems to have attended regularly, were otherwise family affairs, with Georgina Gage, Edward Gage and Sir Rainald and Lady Knightley in attendance. They played bridge in the evenings, sang songs in the Long Gallery, and during the day shot, with bags of 300 pheasants and 50 brace of partridge. They often invited their neighbours, Lord and Lady Hampden. Apparently they all shot better after lunch and drinking champagne. They shot deer in Plashett Wood — at that time owned by my grandfather — duck in the decoy, and snipe in the brooks.

According to Ingram's diary, life at Firle mirrored the lives of aristocratic families prior to the 1914-18 war. The steward Henry Weller, who managed a staff of bricklayers, the stables and coachman, the gardeners, the agricultural workers and the gamekeepers, assisted Ingram. A weekly cheque was cashed at the bank, and Weller appears to have been in charge of paying each different department.

In 1881 Ingram held an audit of the Firle accounts in his room at Firle Place, which all the tenants, the vicar of Firle, and the bankers and solicitors, attended. Lord Gage took the chair and spoke the words that were previously written out for him. He put these into much better English than Ingram had written, but was, poor chap, so painfully shy that he had a job to get the speech out at all. After the audit there were songs.

The halcyon life of Walter Ingram came to an end in 1888 when Douglas Lawrie, an Oxford friend of my grandfather, replaced him, and when I imagine my grandfather regained his self-confidence. This seemed to coincide incidentally with the slump in farm prices, when rents went down to three shillings an acre and farms had to be taken back in hand.

My father appears to have been a much more significant figure than my grandfather. He was Chairman of the local Conservative Party,

Chairman of the County Council, and President of the National Housing Association, and Father of the House of Lords. He can be mentioned in the same frame as Sir John Gage and General Gage in historical importance. Nevertheless he seemed to have inherited the family predilection of being unduly influenced by their choice of agent. Dennis Bush seems to have taken on the mantle of Walter Ingram, and ironically they both lived in the Black House in Firle with a gap of fifty years. Much to my mother's annoyance and dismay, my father followed Dennis Bush's advice meticulously, and his expenditure was supervised at all times. My mother told me that Dennis Bush paid for everything during their honeymoon. As a result of his advice there was precious little left for the family to spend.

Far from gambling or wild living, my father spent much of his income, and that of my mother, on completely inefficient farm buildings and hopeless farm managers — all supervised by Dennis Bush. He seems to have exercised a messianic hold on my father, who treated any criticism of him as a personal affront. For instance I frequently attended farm visits with my father, whose crops were manifestly yielding far less than those of surrounding tenant farmers, but if I were to mention this to my father he would have been mortally insulted. Despite this, we as a family had wonderful childhoods, as both our parents were brilliantly funny, and freedom of speech, if not behaviour, was very much encouraged.

I propose to research a little more of the Gage history that has been omitted from the very commendable history written by my Aunt Yvonne Gage in the 1920s. Aunt Yvonne, one of Cambridge's early under-gra-duettes, wrote a very entertaining scholarly and more or less factual history of Firle and its incumbents. Her book is a family bible and should eventually be published, but it ends in the 19th century and I'm attempting to fill in a few gaps. At some stage my cousin Debo, who knows an immense amount about our family history, may also write about the Gage family. What follows is a summary of the well-established history of the Gage family:-

Sir John Gage (1479-1556) set the benchmark of the Gage family. He built the original Tudor house using the Caen stone which he took from Lewes Priory when he demolished it on the orders of his boss Henry VIII. He clearly was an amazing man, too shrewd to get too close to Henry but still in his circle, and reluctantly agreeing to his divorces (Sir John Gage was a good Catholic). He ended up as Constable of the Tower of London and executor of Henry's will. He was a soldier, a statesman, and a farmer with considerably more acreage that we farm today. He died very conveniently before the accession of Queen Elizabeth I, who had been his prisoner at one stage in the Tower of London and afterwards at Hatfield. His son Edward, as High Sheriff had the unfortunate job of witnessing the burning of the Lewes martyrs during the Protestant purge in the reign of Bloody Mary. After her death the balance changed dramatically against the Catholics, as Elizabeth and her advisors were terrified of a Catholic uprising. For a hundred and fifty years the Gages were threatened with imprisonment and fined. The climate in England changed after the Glorious Revolution of 1689, and the Acts of Settlement of 1701 allowed for religious toleration. The Catholic King James II was replaced by his Protestant daughter Mary and her Dutch husband, William of Orange. Perversely the Gages, along with other members of aristocratic families, became Protestant when it was no longer dangerous to remain a Catholic but merely socially inconvenient. Catholics were excluded from political office, had restrictions on the grandeur of their carriages, and had to send their children to the Douai School run by the Benedictine Douai Abbey community, from where they came back with a non-U accent.

In this new atmosphere life at Firle became more relaxed and frivolous. Sir William Gage (1695-1744), incumbent of Firle between 1713 and 1744 and MP for Seaford from 1727 until his death, was one of the first practitioners of cricket. He organized matches with the Duke of Richmond, and in 1758 Firle Cricket Club (still flourishing) was founded. Sir William commenced the 18th century remodelling of Firle Place which was completed by the first Viscount Gage, who married the beautiful heiress Benedicta Hall, of the romantic Gloucester estate of High Meadow.

He obtained some form of political power, having bought his title on the cheap at Castle Bar in Northern Ireland.

The second viscount married the heiress Elizabeth Gideon, daughter of Sampson Gideon, a powerful banker who saved the government during the South Sea Bubble of 1720. He seems a delightful character, overshadowed somewhat by his more famous brother General Gage, whose exploits in the American War of Independence are well documented. His children did not survive, and the title went to the son of the General and his beautiful American wife Margaret Kemble. He was so absent-minded that he accidentally rode into the wheel of his carriage, which caused his eventual demise.

I remember my father telling me that there was an indoor staff of at least eighteen, organised in a deeply hierarchical household. He remembers a freezing house made warm by the numerous fires attended to by the housemaids. There were many incredibly regimented house parties, with long visits from minor German royalty, and also his cousins the Knightley family. Leila Gage, my Gage grandmother, appears to have been a jolly, rather bossy figure, while her husband seems to have been a retiring, very religious, but endearing figure, whose Tolstoyan habits on one occasion made him lend his coat to the head gardener while he was working in the rain.

As a child my late father seems to have been treated like a king, in a detached childhood with himself and his sisters Rene, Yvonne and Vera being taught by terrifying German governesses, largely away from their parents. Later, when I got to know my aunts, each was entirely different; Rene quite manipulative, Yvonne a totally selfless intellectual, and Vera a rather formidable clairvoyant whose drinks were lethally intoxicating. My grandparents' naivety allowed my father to experiment with dangerous chemicals, making gunpowder unobserved by his non-worldly parents. He went to Eton, was Captain of his Tutors, and was taught by John Christie, an eccentric science master who was distinguished by being the only teacher ever to have his own butler. My father's boyhood came to an abrupt end in the 1914-18 war, when he celebrated his twenty-first birthday in a waterlogged slit trench. During the war both his parents died and the organisation of the house was left to a beautiful cousin, Constance Peel, who was recovering from an unsuccessful love affair with another cousin, Morton Gage. The romance ended when he discovered that the follies of her brother William (who had lost the Peel family £80,000, many millions in today's money, and bankrupted them) meant she would inherit no money.

Having miraculously survived the war after a very serious wound, my father returned to Firle. He parsimoniously pensioned off his three sisters, studied agriculture at Christ Church Oxford, and shared digs with my mother's brother Ivo Grenfell. He convinced the Senior Censor that as he had been nightly patrolling in no-man's land during the war he therefore should get, and got, special permission to escape the Christ Church 10 o'clock curfew. For ten years he lived at Firle as a bachelor, and unsuccessfully courted Lady Elizabeth Bowes-Lyon, the future Queen of England. In 1931 he married my much-feted mother, youngest daughter of Willy and Ettie Desborough, Ettie successfully demolishing all her other suitors.

Nothing has transformed the English social system more than the 1914-18 war, when Victorian certainties were replaced by the doubts that still exist, and which are complicated by the modern technology that is changing all our lives today.

Chapter 6

Anecdotes
Anecdotes from some of the members of the family

THIS MEMOIR IS a personal one and in no way a definitive history of the Gage, Knightley, Grenfell and Peel families, but I think reminiscences are justified for the amusement of future generations.

The main families from which we have descended are coincidentally interlocked. The tomb of Sir John Gage in St. Peter's Church, Firle, is matched in beauty by the tomb of Sir Richard Knightley in St. Mary's Church, Fawsley, and they both lived and managed their estates about the same time. The Gages were Royalists in the civil war and the Knightleys were Roundheads and encouraged the production of the rebellious tracts of Martin Marprelate, which were apparently printed in a secret room at Fawsley Hall above the Oriel window. The fact that Charles hunted before the Battle of Edgehill was a coincidence, and was apparently caused by the Knightleys lending Fawsley Hall to a Royalist friend.

It's a difficult task to get a clear picture of the 3rd, 4th and 5th Viscounts, other than getting the impression of upright Church of England squires who were worthy landlords but who lived half their lives in London and latterly in Whitehall Place. Researching at The Keep (East Sussex Record Office) requires hours of painstaking and not very productive work, but records that at least fifteen indoor staff and nine gardeners kept both houses and gardens ship-shape.

The 3rd Viscount, General Gage's son, seems to have supervised the re-building of Firle village at the end of the 18th century. His successor, the 4th Viscount Henry Hall Gage, succeeded aged eighteen in January

1808. He was educated at Westminster and Trinity College Cambridge, and was a serious mathematician who wrote several mathematical papers which were read before members of the Royal Institution and other scientific societies. He was a friend of the archaeologist Sir Austen Henry Layard, who presented him with a Babylonian bas-relief that was sold by my father. He was such a staunch Conservative, and he and twenty-one other stalwarts voted against a third reading of the Reform Bill in 1832, even after the Duke of Wellington had agreed to it. He was a benign landlord and lowered agricultural rents in the huge agricultural depression after the Napoleonic Wars and the bad harvests, notably in 1829. His son, who predeceased him, was mad on medieval chivalry and his father had revived the game of Quintain, a traditional jousting game. He also attended the Eglinton tournament, which was a financial disaster for the Earl who organised it (read *The Knight and the Umbrella* by Ian Anstruther).

In 1894 my grandfather married Leila Peel and they proceeded to have four children, my father Henry Rainald and my three aunts, Rene, Vera and Yvonne (who, as I previously mentioned, wrote a fine unpublished history of Firle, which I hope to publish one day). I knew my aunts extremely well. They proceeded initially to marry slightly unsatisfactory husbands. Rene, the most formidable of the three, married three times: first to Captain Murray Shuldham-Legh; secondly to Brigadier David Bull with whom she had two children, David (who looked after her and pre-deceased her) and Diana who escaped from her grasp by marrying and emigrating to Canada and who has recently just died (an amazingly nice lady); and thirdly Ernest Tennant, who was at Eton with my Uncle Julian Grenfell. Vera, a stylish woman, whom I liked very much, married a Cambridge don called Frank Birch, who was one of the brains at Bletchley Park solving the Enigma problem. Finally Yvonne — the author of the unpublished *History of Firle* — was a frail, highly intelligent and very selfless lady. She married a penniless guitar player called Adrian van der Horst, and died childless when I was twenty-five.

Photo albums from the time show weekend parties organised by my socially ambitious but slightly parochial Gage grandmother, but on a much lesser scale than those organised by my other grandmother Lady Ettie Desborough, one of the great hostesses of her day (see *Ettie*, a biography by Richard Davenport-Hines).

As previously referred to, Leila's brother William was a quintessential black sheep. Every family has a black sheep and my great-uncle Willy Peel fully deserves such a title. William and Leila's mother, Adelaide Peel, wrote in 1898 of her son's misdeeds, revealed to her by his mother-in-law and a letter from William's father, the Reverend Frederick Peel, in February 1918. By this time William had been put into prison as a result of dishonest dealings in West Virginia in the Peel Splint Coal Company. Newspaper cuttings refer to a statement made at the trial, where Peel is recorded saying: "I can't understand it, it's beyond me – you know I have immense gem mines in the island of Ceylon and my brother is the British Minister to Siam, and here I am in this beastly place." William had eleven

Uncle Willy (Extreme Left)

children, one of whom, his son Charles by his second wife Leonie Hallu, was simply left at a St. Louis hotel and was bought up by a complete stranger. William finally died in suspicious circumstances in Frankfurt on 30th May 1930 aged sixty-seven. I have in my possession many demands for loans to my father, each in sinister but beautifully scripted writing. Whether my grandfather helped to pay William Peel's original debt of £80,000 is completely unproven, but nevertheless in 1888 Laughton Wood was privately sold to William Christie, and the only mention of this in the record office was that he had sold the deer in the wood — which my friend George Christie always told me was to settle a bet.

Another allegedly black sheep was my grandfather's sister, The Hon. Selina Gage, who married a cantankerous member of the Taylor family. He caught her in a compromising position in the sitting room at Chyknell Hall with a man who was not her husband. Her husband immediately divorced her and absorbed her considerable marriage endowment, after which she was rather unfairly ostracised and wiped from the annals of her family. It says something for the Victorian morality in the late 19th century that Selina was then entirely airbrushed out of the family; and never again spoken to by her daughters, who referred to her as a Mrs White. All photos of her were obliterated; save one found in a negative form by Michael Tollemache, who is currently writing a history of Chyknell and who discovered it.

My great-grandmother, Sophia Selina Knightley, married Henry Gage, who, as mentioned, pre-deceased his father Henry Hall. Like the Cowpers, the Knightleys died out by failing to produce male heirs, so that the Fawsley Estate passed to my father in 1938 and the Panshanger Estate passed to my grandmother in 1907. Rather like the Gages, the direct line of inheritance has been broken by innumerable cousins who have taken on the incumbency of both estates. In the famous painting by Zoffany of the English Grand Tour collectors, there is one of the buyers, a Knightley, coincidentally alongside the famous collector the 3rd Earl Cowper. Firle was re-modelled with great finesse in the 18th century. Sadly, the grandiose plans for the re-modelling of Fawsley Hall coincided with the worst practices of the Victorian period. Lord Knightley simultaneously built ugly wings spoiling the architecture and sold off a portion of the estate to pay for the honour of a visit by Queen Victoria. As mentioned, he was allegedly such a snob that Addison lampooned him by exchanging the word 'nightly' in 'nightly to the listening earth repeats the glory of its birth' to 'Knightley'.

After Lord Knightley's death in 1895 his son Sir Valentine lived in Fawsley and Sir Henry lived in little Fawsley. They were both charming fox hunting squires, and Sir Charles, their father, was a frequent visitor to Firle. Sir Charles's wife Lady Louisa was a modern woman, a feminist and a political mover and shaker, and Sir Henry's wife was so envious of her that when eventually he inherited Fawsley Hall all the furniture and pictures in the house were sold, possibly out of spite. My father inherited Fawsley in 1938 in an almost derelict state.

The Cowpers were a fascinating family who lived for three hundred years at the Panshanger estate in Hertfordshire. The 1st Earl was the architect of the Act of Union between England and Scotland in 1707, and made the family fortune as Chancellor of the Exchequer for Queen Anne, and the subsequent Earls married well. The Cowpers became an enormously rich and influential family. The 3rd Earl created one of the most important art collections in England, being advised by Zoffany and living most of his life in Florence. The 5th Earl built Panshanger, which overlooked the park designed by Repton. The 6th and 7th Earls divided their time between Panshanger and Wrest Park, and when the 7th Earl (Uncle Francis) died childless in 1905 it was inherited by his niece, my grandmother, Lady Ettie Desborough.

Several pictures from the famous Panshanger collection are hung at Firle. The star picture at Firle is indeed the Van Dyck. The Earl of Grantham's brother, Willem, bought back the family painting which had been lost through the spoils of war, as Willem's son pre-deceased him, and the Van Dyck was then inherited by his brother the Earl of Grantham. In turn the Earl of Grantham's daughter inherited the group portrait and she married the 2nd Earl Cowper, so thereafter this canvas came down through the Cowper family line. The 4th Earl only survived his father by ten years, as he died in 1799, but managed somehow to save the collection from the executors of his father's estate. His younger brother, who married Emily Lamb, sadly demolished the old house at Cole Green and constructed the gothic revival house Panshanger which was built between 1807 and 1820 from the designs of Samuel Wyatt and William Atkinson, and the park was established under the supervision of Henry Repton. He added to the collection and indeed added the picture gallery to house the Grantham pictures, the Rembrandt and his father's Italian purchases. The 6th Earl lived mainly at Wrest Park, but rebuilt Panshanger after the 1850's fire and built the Orangery, which is still standing, and the gardens. He was an MP for Canterbury and Lord Lieutenant of Kent, and died in 1856. The 7th and last Earl Cowper was a liberal politician, who was born in 1834 and died in 1905. He was Lord Lieutenant for Ireland, a Privy Counsellor and first chairman of the Hertfordshire County Council in the 1880s. Both Earls were generous benefactors in and around Hertford. The entire collection was bequeathed to my grandmother Lady Desborough, as she was Ettie's Uncle Francis's favourite niece. My grandmother Ettie married William Henry Grenfell, who later became Lord Desborough and owner of Taplow Court, Buckinghamshire — now a Buddhist Centre — which had been purchased in 1852 by his grandfather Charles Pascoe Grenfell. Pascoe Grenfell was also a collector, and purchased two paintings by Philip de Koninck, one of which now hangs at the National Gallery, Trafalgar Square, which was sold in lieu to pay for my mother's death duties. Another depletion was by the sale of a major Fra Bartolomeo 'Holy Family' to the Getty Museum to endow Firle Place, and a Correggio 'Head of Christ' to cover my losses at Lloyd's of London. In common with many I joined Lloyd's in a somewhat haphazard way, and it was by luck rather than good judgement that my losses were considerable rather than disastrous. As a result, I sold the Correggio 'Head of Christ' bequeathed to me (chosen by Diana) with a large value to the Getty Museum, and after tax much of this went on meeting my losses. I'm not proud that I allowed some of the money to slip out of my hands, on top of losses as a result of which I had to sell my house in London, which could so easily have been avoided.

Because of the tragedies of the two Desborough sons being killed in the First World War and their third son Ivo losing his life in a road accident, the works of art were divided by my mother and her sister Monica Salmond, and some of them hang at Firle. It seems curious in this modern age to think that two large houses were only partially lived in for long periods of the 19th Century, as the Cowpers seemed to live largely at Wrest Park and the Gages were in London for the season.

Chapter 7
Second Time Round

In 2003 I met Alex Templeton at Lord Skidelsky's cocktail party. I remember Alex's intense eyes making a great impression, and a feeling of sadness when she disappeared before the lunch. We made contact shortly afterwards and I met her at her beach cottage in Seaford, where she was writing a novel that is still to be published.

I had reluctantly accepted my wife Diana's divorce documents a year earlier and therefore was technically free though still in an unofficial, but mutually agreeable, relationship with the cartoonist Nikki Bass who would fight hard but honourably to keep hold of me.

For the next five years Alex and I did much travelling together; to Mount Ararat, to France, a ferocious riding holiday from Arequipa to the Pacific coast over the Atacama Desert — the driest spot in the world — and we decided to get married in 2008. Alex for some reason at the age of thirty-eight had never before been married. Valentine was born in 2009, and it took me at least five years to come round to beginning a new family at seventy-two years old — a feat that had been successfully achieved by Sir Charles Tennant in the 19th century and Charlie Chaplin in the 20th.

Becoming one of the oldest fathers in England has been a wonderful but 'kill or cure' experience for myself, my dear wife, and also my relationship with Henry and Ben, whose philosophical acceptance of having such a young brother is something for which I will always be grateful.

Our travels have continued after our marriage and, accompanied by our young son Valentine, we have been to Mongolia, the Amazon, and China, about which I wrote the following for the Firle Parish magazine:

Holiday in the Land of Genghis Khan- By Lord Gage
Appeared in the local parish magazine September 2014

In the 13th century Mongolia, most of China and some of Tibet were ruled by Genghis Khan. Since then Mongolia has been diminished in the 20th century by both Russia and China, but is even now at least twice as big as England so some idea of the size of his empire can be envisaged. In the six weeks that Alex, Valentine and I were there, we merely scratched the surface. In Ulaanbaatar we were met by Adiya, an intelligent English-speaking Mongolian camel expert. In his company we drove 3,000 kilometres, visiting Khosvgol, the second largest freshwater lake in the world. There we met a Shaman (a holy man) who performed an amazing ritual with us.

In Southern Mongolia we drove many hundreds of kilometers over a vast hilly plateau (slightly reminiscent of the South Downs), and every fifty miles or so we came across a nomadic village, and every hundred miles a small town.. We went through a tiny bit of the Gobi Desert where the tracks seemed to be totally unmapped. When at a loss, our driver drove to the nearest nomad, perhaps a mile away on the neighbouring hilltop, who obligingly pointed us in the right direction!

Buddhism is once more on the rise after its appalling persecution by the communists in the late 1940's when many thousands of Buddhist monks were killed. In the desert we attended a Buddhist temple which reminded me slightly of Firle Church, since the locals came many miles to make their devotions. Back in Ulaanbaatar, in an affluent suburb, we met a high-ranking Buddhist priest called Rinpoche who was charming, spoke good English and was unexpectedly articulate about current affairs for a man who had spent the last three years in solitary meditation in a cave. He was reminiscent of a young Anglican bishop.

Scenically, the Tibetan part of China is equally spectacular, and we saw more beauty in a month than I normally see in a year, but the relaxed atmosphere of the newly freed Mongolia was replaced by a slight unease, as Chinese Szechuan is not democratic.

The problem of preparing for fatherhood again at an advanced age was complicated by the opinion of my other children, who at first were anxious and were filled with the unwarranted foreboding that my new young wife would quickly divorce me in a multi-million pound divorce settlement, a conviction fostered by my ex-wife Diana, who was certain that incidents in her own life were about to be repeated — as her own much married parents had split up with dire consequences for all. It's understandable that my children may have thought so, with a thirty-seven year gap; but divorce doesn't appear to be in Alex's mind-set.

No one can exaggerate the complexities of having a father seventy-five years older than yourself, but so far so good. Apart from the companionship to anyone living in a medium sized stately home, one of the many benefits that Alex has brought to our family is that she is the antidote to the family curse of alcohol. My mother and brother suffered from this horrible disease — and I and my ex Diana, without actually being alcoholics, certainly drank too much, with the resulting errors in judgement. Presently my own consumption has at least halved. Alex's own example of total abstinence is a much-needed alternative to the entire family.

As a lot of my life has consisted of trying to look after my three sons, a brief mention should be made of them. In a film on Winston Churchill his father came to him in a dream, talked about his own life, and as an afterthought asked his son how his painting had progressed. This suggests that he completely underestimated the fact that his son had become one of the most important political figures in history. I therefore would like to mention the fact that I'm very proud of my three children, and they may well become distinguished in their own right in later life. For the last forty years I seem to have been ferrying them about in different directions, sometimes driving irresponsibly — especially when I lost my temper feeling heat in the back seat, and when I stopped the car realised that Henry and Ben had lit a small fire in the compartment in the back. I gave them a dressing down and then exceeded the speed limit, only to be pulled up by a policeman — and was told by my children that I'd been very naughty.

It is a continuing joy to follow my three children's careers. Although Valentine now engages most of my attention, I'm still conscious that children of all ages need as much encouragement as possible, and I'm delighted that Henry is showing such an interest at Firle. I am equally pleased that Ben has taken on the mantle at Fawsley, and has married such a lovely girl, Natasha. And I believe that Valentine, thirty-five years their junior, will also make a substantial contribution, as he shows all the signs that he'll make his parents proud. He is already a considerable artistic talent.

Parenting is so entirely different nowadays, when children have to be seen and heard, to the detriment of their parents' ego. Parenting courses are now more or less compulsory, even though I did laugh at the cartoon when a hen-pecked husband says how much he is enjoying the parenting classes as it enables him to get away from his children. Parents now seem to spend most of their free time watching their children play games, when parents of my generation came to watch me once a year — but this was conventional at that time. I suppose this was a hangover from the Victorian era, when stiff upper lip values inhibited intimate relationships. I indeed know of some people of my own age who were never once visited by their parents during their entire boarding school experience. Equality between parent and child was not an option in my childhood, but now thankfully it has at last become the norm.

On one occasion in Henry's and Ben's childhood, when we had an inter-house telephone at Firle, I happened to overhear Henry discussing with Ben the merits of a particularly expensive German Riesling which I'd hidden in the cellar and which he'd taken, aged twelve, without any form of parental consent. It was difficult for him to deny that he'd stolen it, but I did compliment him on his choice. Henry's achievement of getting into Bristol was helped by his godfather, Sebastian Grigg, telling me that all he had to do to get a place was to go to see the admissions tutor. In those days I was no longer living with Diana so I left a message on the answering machine. I was delighted to hear Henry's voice saying: "Dad, I know I just have to get up early and go and see the admissions tutor and not take no for an answer." The admissions tutor, who'd never been approached before in this manner, was so amazed that he awarded Henry a place for his initiative, papering over the fact that Henry's A-level results were not as good as they should have been due to spending most of his time with a Dutch girlfriend.

Ben has been a late developer, but has shown huge determination in continuing the responsibility of enhancing the Fawsley estate. He has not been exactly tactful in his relationship with his trustees, a trait which he must have inherited from me. But nevertheless, preservation of that beautiful and derelict estate is well under way, and soon to be augmented by the contribution from his new wife Natasha.

It's very surprising at the age of eighty-five to be engaged once again in school runs and the continuous involvement in the day-to-day education of another child. Luckily parenting is a sort of freemasonry, and parents of half my age seem to have taken my advanced years with great tolerance, though often I'm mistaken as Valentine's grandfather. But it is an enormously rewarding experience to be talking once again to fellow parents about guiding Valentine in the same way that I did thirty years ago for my older children, including the difficult decisions about further schooling and, just as before, the intimidating financial challenges that these bring. This does have a great social handicap, since quite often school becomes more important than other social responsibilities. Luckily my older sons are able and willing to help out. Recently my forty year old son Ben took my place at an important commemorative dinner in honour of my grandfather Lord Desborough, while I attended the Cumnor School production of 'Jack and the Bean Stalk' in which Valentine played a leading role.

Valentine shows impressive promise with excellent school reports, which he hides under a 'dead pan' expression (fashionable in modern day school). He can be alternatively taciturn or ultra-talkative, and one is only aware that he is acutely observant and attentive by the odd stray remark, which confirms he is following outside conversation. He's shown a degree of natural artistic talent and has also exhibited thespian skills, which he displayed in the masterful three-minute speech he gave at Alex's fiftieth birthday in front of politicians, university lecturers and famous artists. He did so with flawless aplomb, and was congratulated on his delivery by a BBC newsreader. I'm very lucky to have another very interesting son, who is a credit to both myself and his mother.

Every incumbent has had an impact on Firle. Sir John Gage built the Tudor Hall; Sir William and the 1st Viscount changed the outside of the house completely and added the long gallery; and the 5th Viscount added the pine staircase. My mother brought in a sizeable amount of the famous Cowper collection of paintings and china when her mother died in 1952. My stepmother added bathrooms. Diana changed the kitchen radically and the old-fashioned staffing regime; while my dear wife, Alex, has added a door — miraculously overcoming stringent planning rules — to connect the kitchen with the garden, and she has also created a magnificent herb garden, and re-invigorated the administration of the house with a discerning eye, re-creating the lived-in feeling that makes a historic house a comfortable home as well as an attraction for the visitors.

Firle has been twice burgled, once in 1950 when the entire contents of the safe — which included some valuable jewellery — were taken in the middle of the night. At that time security hardly existed. For instance, the key to the safe was kept in a drawer in the dining room and its whereabouts was probably common knowledge, although no blame has ever been suggested regarding any of my father's staff. I remember that for days afterwards my mother patrolled the corridors carrying an enormous cudgel, hoping the burglars would return. The second burglary occurred in July 2009, when much more sophisticated security had been installed. I happened to be in the house the night this happened, at the same time as a High Court judge, his clerk and his entourage (Firle remains an Occasional Judges Lodgings during the County Assizes courts). A very accomplished burglar realised that the security cameras were not fixed on two particular china cabinets, and amongst the thirty pieces of china stolen there happened to be two immensely important Sèvres vases, valued at half a million pounds each. How he managed to creep into the house, remove these large and fragile pieces of china without breaking them, and clean up his DNA remains a complete mystery. We surmised that he visited the house as a member of the public and noticed there was no security on these particular cabinets.

Very unusually — and almost miraculously — the most important pieces have been returned to us as a result of an elaborate sting operation organised by the Yorkshire police, where a similar burglary had occurred, and the prisoner is still I believe in jail. The burglar's iPhone revealed that he had made a call on it at the time of the burglary from Firle Park. Although the burglary was hurtful, one has to admire the skill with which it was carried out, and we are indeed grateful that thanks to the police these historic and treasured pieces are now back at Firle.

It is difficult to make changes when past generations have set so much in stone. For instance, the downstairs drawing room was designed specifically to house the family portraits. However, innovation has to occur to enable the house to continue as a viable enterprise. Plans are afoot to reverse the main entrance for the family to the back door, and access to the front to enable commercial enterprise to maintain the fabric. The riding school will be used as a venue for weddings and filming, and the south garden and the park for various fairs and events.

Sir John Gage, soldier and statesman, was above all a businessman. He sold his wool in the great hall and would have approved of any family venture that would enable the Gage family to continue to live in the house that he built and 'adored'.

Alex and I have lived from 2006 till 2019 at Firle doing squirearchy — hunting, organising shooting parties, having celebratory birthday parties, carol services for the village and generally keeping the house alive. We now plan to move out, enabling my son Henry — the heir — to move into the other half (in keeping with modern practice), while we live half the week in the charming farmhouse Bushy Lodge where I grew up as a child, though for the time being we will keep rooms in part of Firle Place.

The last part of my life, although I am semi-retired, seems as active as the first part. Being a father of three sons (of slightly different age groups admittedly) is a full-time affair. A younger son demands more concentration, much less alcohol on my part, and more activity, as parenting has become a very full-time affair. Nowadays every parent is hands on. The drawn-out family holidays of my childhood, which I've previously discussed, were testing, as is the co-running of the two estates in partnership with my elder children.

There are still feudal touches at Firle, one of them being my own eightieth birthday celebrations in the riding school to which the village were invited. More recently we celebrated my wife Alex's fiftieth birthday, which triumphantly took place in the Great Hall with a marquee outside, where two hundred and fifty people applauded Alex's eloquent speech. These included completely separate bands of friends who came from spiritual, hunting and artists, including her family and previous boyfriend. Everybody dressed up in Amazonian costume, and it went on long after I personally had gone to bed.

A year later there was a wonderfully successful wedding in Firle Church and the Great Hall celebrating the marriage of my second son Ben to Natasha Llewellyn, which included a memorable luncheon interspersed with elegant speeches and much revelry on the South Lawn, where the sun chose to shine to provide a perfect day.

Ben Gage and Tash Llewellyn at their wedding at St. Peter's, Firle 2019

Lord Gage's Speech for Alex's Birthday

Alan Moorehead sadly had a stroke and he could only say two things:-

'Bloody Awful' — the next was 'Bloody Marvellous'.

I've only got one thing to say tonight, my marriage to Alex is (long pause) BLOODY MARVELLOUS!

Can every one sit down and drink her health on her fiftieth birthday.

Alex's Birthday Speech

Nicky — thank you for those sweet words, as so often they were few in number, but perfectly made — and by the way I'm not about to return the compliment as Nicky said it would make him cringe — so I won't say what I'm not allowed to say, but I will say that I also have a wonderful son, wonderful friends, wonderful family and a wonderful extended family. Valentine, Ben and Henry, how lucky you all are in your very different ways to have inherited some of Nicky's better qualities. Namely his likeability, his quirkiness and his generosity.

In a few weeks' time my mother will be eighty. Mum, your fierce intelligence, your courage and determination has and still is a source of great inspiration. Can we stay seated, but I would all like to raise a glass to her. To Ann Templeton. Thank you everybody and thank you mum.

Martin Amis has a line about reaching fifty and suddenly realising that maybe for the first time we have a past. Unfortunately I think I had a past a little earlier than this, but I'm happy to say that a lot of my past is represented here in this room tonight. Thank you all for coming, and thank you especially to those of you who have come from far away — to those of you who have flown down from Scotland, flown from New York, flown in from Spain and from the

North. One of our DJs flew in yesterday from Southern India to be here, and another of our DJs, my brother, Ed Templeton and his family flew in from Sri Lanka yesterday also. Also there are quite a few of you that I have not seen for far too long, and it's very good to see you.

I confess I've had more than a single moment's anguish about this party — I've had many moments of anguish about this party, in fact there have been many emergency trustees meetings in order to discuss this party — and I can see Jonathan Gage saying, 'It's true!'

I have felt rather uncertain about combining my different friends and my different pasts. My meditating, more spiritual friends, who don't drink, or who hardly drink at all. My hunting friends, and my artist friends who almost definitely drink too much; and my molecular science friends and god knows how much they drink.

Years ago I was commissioned to write a novel and what I wrote was a fictional story, but fifteen years later a lot of what I wrote has come true in my life. I'm not going to illustrate that here, but the point is that perhaps with the benefit of hindsight, the benefit of the passage of time, or the benefit of now being incredibly old, I can see that the truth is both fiction and stranger than fiction.

And finally a brief word about Edwardian Amazonian…. last year Nicky, Valentine and I travelled to the Amazon. At one point we found ourselves in the frontier town of Manaus, and in the middle of Manaus in the middle of a pretty dense jungleness, lawlessness, is a pretty old Edwardian opera house, with red velvet seats and an amazing stucco ceiling and rather a lot of Edwardian charm and Edwardian elegance — and you might say Edwardian raffishness, and you might say that it was this that inspired the theme for this evening and how charming, elegant and beautiful you all look….. and one or two rather raffish.

No birthday party can be about anything other than the past, but let's make tonight about the present and I really hope you all have a wonderful evening.

Valentine's Speech for Alex's Birthday

I just want to say a few words about my mum…

She's rather peculiar, but not in a bad way, rather like a fantastic beast, and she writes lots of silly stories about goblins, seagulls and curves.

She's very caring towards animals, plants and human beings. In fact we all are….. I especially care for horses and dad especially

cares for (long pause) fish!

My mum is always taking me to India, on her phone and talking about feelings. She's brilliant but perhaps a bit too bossy.

Now can we all sing Happy Birthday to her again!

Valentine giving a speech at Alex's 50th Birthday Party

There are a mass of things that need to be done in order to maintain an estate. All are common sense, but without direction they would not happen. Tree planting, the drainage of the long pond and the decoy pond, the continued re-roofing of the houses on the estate and especially the roof of Firle Place, is the responsibility of both the incumbent and the agent. There is also constant pressure to strike a balance between the expense of maintaining the house without over-commercialisation. Likewise, it is important to ensure that the estate's rental policy does not damage the structure of the village by making properties unaffordable, and not too pernicious to make it impossible for local people to live in houses which they took on when the rental policy was less commercial. At the same time the reality is that an estate needs a good rental income in order to finance necessary maintenance and improvements. This is not a slide rule exercise, and requires both sympathy and entrepreneurial skills.

I'm hoping to write Volume 2 over the next few years, so my life with Alex and Valentine will be a forthcoming edition. But as these brief memoirs might be considered a template for future incumbents it is important to add the essential role of the incumbent's wife, for Firle dies without a feminine touch. Besides being a senior lecturer at Brighton University and a budding entrepreneur for exotic products, Alex has devoted much of her time to organising a medium-sized stately home. This includes the minutiae of sorting out pictures, hygiene, the matching of lights, bedrooms, the delicate issues of staffing a house which is divided between the private side and the public side, managing the gardens department and adding the lustre of a herb garden, to name just a few of the huge benefits of a partnership with a lady whose social skills are up to the rigours of a stately home. This is just as important as my joint governance, with my son, of the Firle Estate outside the house.

We now have a full-time events secretary who works with Henry to organise our weddings, film and fashion shoots, antique fairs, horse trials, *Son et Lumières*, television bookings, such as 'Bake Off, the Professionals', full-length feature films, conferences and, with the redevelopment of the stables, many other money-making events. There are also additional possibilities of increasing the housing in a responsible manner to encourage the wellbeing of the estate, which includes the pub, the village shop, and Firle Church of England Primary School, all of which are so important for the community. There is a housing shortage in the area, which means there is a requirement and an opportunity to increase the amount of housing in Firle and the neighbouring villages in a responsible manner — and certainly not the mass development so beloved of estate agents and politicians, where the character of a village would be demolished by becoming too large. Somehow these problems were solved differently and more successfully by our forebears, who for some reason achieved more beautiful buildings with far less technical advantages.

No one can look into the future, but I hope our family will show the gift of survival, which my forebears have displayed.

Chapter 8
Dogs, Horses, Friends and Ideas

I AM ENJOYING quite a long life, punctuated and up to a point dominated by family, dogs, horses and friends. Dogs have played an important part in my life. As their lives are so much shorter than humans the love of possessing them is tempered by the poignancy of losing them, but as Axel Munthe writes in *The Story of Saint Michele*, the only way to get over the loss of a dog is to get another one.

My mother had a very neurotic dog called Sharky, who we loved as children and who died during the war. My grandparents had Chows. My introduction to dog owning was in 1960, when I chose a particularly intelligent but slightly demonic sheep dog who as a six month old puppy rounded up a large herd of cattle. He used to disappear at regular intervals. Once, when confined to the house due to complaints from neighbours from his unwanted advances to their dogs, he tricked me by opening a window in the afternoon and then disappearing at night to achieve a conquest three miles away. Eventually he accidentally bit the end of my finger off when I unwisely interfered in a dogfight. In retrospect he dominated me.

My next dog was a rather aimless Golden Labrador called Simba, but ownership came into the fore when I was introduced by Juliet Townsend to the Clumber Spaniel. I learnt about the breed when I was told to walk a Clumber Spaniel round a class in a dog show. When interviewed by the judge, I could only say that I knew nothing about them apart from the fact they were very charming. Since then and to the present day Firle has been occupied by many generations of a big family of Clumber Spaniels. So far we have had six Clumbers: Juno, Phoebe, Jupiter, Firle, Percy and

83

Ganymede. Percy and Jupiter sadly died, but their mother Phoebe still staggers on and we're about to get another.

Horses have always played a significant role in my life, a lot of which I inherited from my mother. Apparently she used to compete in point-to-point races riding side saddle in the 1920s, a feat that my less experienced father himself copied, although on one occasion he allegedly stopped in the middle of a race when his hat fell off. All my life I've ridden — first of all on my favourite horse Augustus, half thoroughbred, half carthorse. Later he was succeeded by Frumity, Golden Eye, Sable, Hughie, King, and at the present moment Pi. Quite unknowingly I was encouraged in a charming way by Richard Meade, who had been a triple Olympic gold medallist. His modesty contrasted with another distinguished rider who put me in my place when I was out shooting with a local friend John Sclater. He explained he had won the Fox Hunter chase and had ridden several times in the Grand National, which ended my conversation about hunting. The enthusiasm that I have inherited from my mother has been shared both by Alex, who is a very confident dressage enthusiast, but also by my young son Valentine, and I'm hopeful that we'll all be hunting together on my eighty-sixth birthday.

C. R. M. Routh, my tutor at Eton, once wrote in my report that he did not know whether or not I would be successful in life but I would always have many friends. I have indeed enjoyed the friendship of very many, amongst whom have been: Anthony Grigg, Garry Runciman, Fionn Morgan, Caroline Cranbrook, George and Mary Christie and their children, Lindy Dufferin, John Fairbairn, Robert Loder, Chris and Primrose Arnander, Robin Gage, Vanessa Williams-Ellis and Ian Rankin to name a few — and of course my direct family.

I have been fortunate to have travelled fairly extensively, starting with my parents who took us to Greece and elsewhere in Europe. Later I went on an adventurous trek with Diana to find Ciudad Perdida, the lost city in Colombia, visited Machu Picchu in Peru on three separate occasions with different companions, and went on an expedition to Papua New Guinea with a girlfriend Sophie Hicks, whose ambitious plans didn't quite take in the risks involved in travelling in that under-developed country. More recently there are the amazing adventures with Alex and Valentine that I have mentioned previously.

Historically the period between 1945 and the present day has been free of war, unlike the preceding fifty years where my father faced and took part in two terrible world wars. We are so far indeed fortunate.

Nowadays the standard of living is immensely more luxurious for nearly everyone. For most of us living in Europe and much of the rest of the world, the problem is not poverty but the bewildering freedom of choice, while at the same time the gap between the 'haves' and 'have nots' becomes wider and wider. I'm in agreement with my father's advice, that any incumbent of Firle should count their blessings.

I am fortunate to have the security of a happy marriage. I am hopeful of seeing Valentine progress into manhood. Though I'll be eighty-seven when he goes to public school, I'm excited at the prospect of watching his progress there, and even afterwards at university, and of witnessing the fulfilment of the careers of my older sons Henry and Ben.

Chapter 9

The Future

HENRY, BEN AND VALENTINE are all going to need each other in the future, and I know that they will love each other and that Firle and Fawsley will be in safe hands.

As Alex mentioned in her speech the three of them have inherited some of my better qualities.

Sir John Gage provided a template for the future, and this seems to have guided the Gages down the centuries. His will — which I will repeat verbatim — is to me personally moving, and his words as relevant and perceptive today as they were five hundred years ago. In his will Sir John directed that 'a tuppeny dole should be given to all such poor persons that had come to his funeral besides giving alms to all neighbouring parishes.' In payment for this, he directed that his gold collar of the Order of the Garter should be sold and his blue Mantel of the Order be presented to the college of Windsor. He also directed that a chantry should be maintained in the church at Firle for evermore, and that the chantry priest 'being obedient and serviceable' to his heirs and successors, should have meat, drink and lodgings in his manor house of West Firle. He also charged his heirs 'to maintain and keep hospitality without which stop and a store of household stuff the testator feared they would be greatly hindered in their living.'

Yvonne Gage adds that in all his letters as in this, his last will, one sees Sir John's love of Firle. He seems almost movingly proud of it. 'You know I have a poor house in Firle' is a sentence which occurs in a letter he sent asking Cromwell to give him confiscated monastic land — using the pretext that Firle is a very poor house to back up his rising position in Henry VIII's court. I am glad to think he died in his beloved house, and was buried where he wished. Mark Lower (possibly a contemporary) says of him: 'he was undoubtedly the most popular county man of his time.'

Timeline for Henry Nicolas Gage, 8th Viscount Gage

1895   Birth of father, **Henry** Rainald Gage, 6th Viscount Gage

1905   Birth of mother, Alexandra **Imogen** Clair Grenfell

1931   Marriage of parents on 26th February

1932   Birth of George John St. Clere (**Sammy**) Gage, 7th Viscount Gage, on 8th July

1934   Birth of Henry **Nicolas** Gage, 8th Viscount Gage, on 9th April

1937   Hon. **Camilla** Gage's birth, on 2th July

1939   World War II starts

1940   Evacuation from Firle — Norfolk — Wales

1942   St. George's Choir School, Windsor

1943   Highfield Prep School

1947   Eton

1952   Oxford, National Service

1960   C. Tennant & Sons, Reading College, Fawsley

1965   Camilla marries **Ed**ward Cazalet

1969   Death of mother

1971   Sammy marries Valerie **Ann** Dutch (divorced 1975)

1971   Father marries **Diana** Campbell-Gray (died 1992)

1974   Marriage to Lady **Diana** Beatty

1975   Birth of **Henry**, 25th June

1977   Birth of **Ben**edict, 21st February

1982   Death of father

1990   Sammy marries **Deirdre** Kingsbury

1993   Death of Sammy

1997   Divorce from Diana

2009   Marriage to **Alex**andra Templeton. Birth of **Valentine**.